The Most PC for Your Money

By Tina Rathbone

alpha
books

A Division of Prentice Hall Computer Publishing
11711 North College, Carmel, Indiana 46032 USA

Alpha Books, 11711 N. College Ave., Carmel, IN 46032

International Standard Book Number:1-56761-006-4

Library of Congress Catalog Card Number: 92-82729

95 94 93 92   8 7 6 5 4 3 2 1

Interpretation of the printing code: the rightmost number of the first series of numbers is the year of the book's printing; the rightmost number of the second series of numbers is the number of the book's printing. For example, a printing code of 92-1 shows that the first printing of the book occurred in 1992.

Printed in the United States of America.

Trademarks

Publisher
Marie Butler-Knight

Managing Editor
Elizabeth Keaffaber

Product Development Manager
Lisa A. Bucki

Acquisitions Editor
Susan Klopfer

Development Editor
Faithe Wempen

Senior Production Editor
Linda Hawkins

Manuscript Editor
San Dee Phillips

Cover and Interior Illustrations
Steve Vanderbosch

Designer
Bill Hendrickson

Indexer
Hilary Adams

Special thanks to McCarter for ensuring
the technical accuracy of this book.

To Andy, Maria and Laptop.

Tina Rathbone, former editor of Supercomputing Review *magazine, lives, works and fishes off the pier with her husband, Andy, in Ocean Beach, California.*

Steve Vanderbosch, artist, doesn't have any pets and really likes to vacation with his wife Julie. He also likes to snow ski, bike ride, and swim.

Contents

Foreword

Having relied on my own sage-like wisdom and comparison-shopping prowess to purchase the wrong computer three times out of three, I feel eminently qualified to comment on the importance of Tina Rathbone's latest opus, *The Most PC for Your Money.*

Close friends have never described me as being overly conservative, thrifty, or prudent. They usually just leave it at tight-fisted dwarf. Then again, they are the kind of people who would allow me to rank them among my close friends, so what judgment could they possibly possess?

I, for one, do not consider it cheap to actually use the multitudinous Buy One, Get One Free coupons that proliferate daily in my mailbox. Nor do I shun the lesser-known, inexpensive beer in favor of fancy brands merely because the outcast's yellow label sports the word generic.

For those who would bend for an orphaned gutter penny, or check the coin-return slot of a public phone before dialing, or consult the grocery store's Cost Per Unit pricing guide before purchasing that generic beer, there is now deliverance from the price-traps and ambiguity of computer shopping.

All too often I've called upon one of the many wondrous and sophisticated computers at the Rathbone residence, only to return in head-hung shame to my floppy-disked dinosaur; my aged-but-faithful Commodorus Rex having replaced my T.I.-rodactyl, which followed my Atari-opithecus.

I watched each amble toward extinction as software offerings at the computer store dwindled—supplanted by more-adaptable IBM programs. Whether a cataclysmic event killed off the great beasts that reside in my computer room, or mere inability to adapt to a changing technology did them in, is unknown. All I know is, in the time it takes me to load one program, other computers can derivate pi to the googolplexic decimal, hack a line into my personal American Express account, and fax out for pizza.

So, it is with a happy heart that I welcome into the world Tina's how-to guide on computer consuming. Armed with it, I can readily stand before throngs of commission-hungry computer store clerks—the type who appear to have been formerly employed in selling used cars, but who perhaps had too much conscience for that trade.

Though I still don't know a megabyte from a Vegematic, I know I can take this guide into any computer store, hold it aloft in Damoclean fashion before a cowering sales force, and demand the respect I deserve.

Because I was allowed to read the rough draft, I get to see the book before it hits the stores at a bargain price. I know I'd have to rent rooms in my home to itinerant field laborers to afford comparable computer advice.

So for those of you reading this while hiding behind the pet-care book rack and hoping the clerk doesn't jump out with a "May I help you?" or a "Dis ain't no library, ya know?"—read on. The clerk's probably at lunch or something, and you haven't even gotten to the good part yet.

Better yet, buy the book and take it home.

Awaiting you is a veritable sea of hints on computer shopping, ordering by mail, obtaining technical support, adding on accessories, and generally figuring out what the machine can actually do. Most importantly, you'll learn that "inexpensive" need not mean "cheap." And, lest I forget, it makes a great gift for those hard-to-buy-for friends and relatives who are always mentioning that some day, maybe, they'd like to perhaps buy a computer.

Enjoy.

Andrew Kleske
July, 1992

Introduction

Welcome to the ranks of computer shoppers, where people fall into two categories.

The first type of shopper considers a computer system to be a whole package. It comes with this amount of memory, that size of hard drive; this monitor, that chip. These shoppers compare various systems, weigh advantages and disadvantages, and finally buy the package that fits their needs and wallets.

Blue-Plate Special Shoppers Crave Convenience

In a restaurant, this shopper orders the blue-plate special. These blue-plate shoppers know that the dealer has made many of the computer-buying decisions for them. They trust the overall result will be satisfactory, like a well-balanced meal.

Maybe you're the blue-plate special shopper. If buying a system already configured sounds like you, keep reading.

The software chapters in this book will help you figure out what computing tasks you'd like your new system to accomplish. Then you can communicate your needs to the dealer. Scan the hardware chapters to see the big picture.

Easy-to-Spot Icons Help Blue-Plate-Special Shoppers Home-in on Helpful Buying Tips and Secrets

- **Jargon Busters** sprinkled throughout this book prepare you for the lingo you'll encounter while shopping.

- **Bottom Line** tips help you compare systems at a glance.

- **Historical Figures** detail the story behind a component. (Once you get your computer home, you may even find yourself peeking at these sections, curious to learn more!)

- **Notes** point out ways to do things with a bit more savvy.

- The **Glossary** helps it all make sense.

The À la Carte Shopper

The other type of shopper takes the modular approach. This shopper considers one component—the motherboard, for instance—and mentally adds other components, only after weighing their individual merits.

The new system's hard drive capacity must complement the memory architecture; both will meld with microprocessor power. The new monitor will target specific graphics needs, which also might require a graphics accelerator board. (All of these components will be explained in their own chapters inside the book!)

Many, many decisions await these shoppers—as do hours of fascinating study for each component they wish to buy.

It's easy to imagine this type of shopper in a restaurant, querying the waiter for details on each menu item—then ordering several dishes, à la carte. It may take more time and trouble, but à la carte shoppers feel that the final result—a computer system designed to fit their unique requirements—is worth it.

If eating à la carte is your idea of fun, this book can be your guide to putting together the best PC system for your money.

- You'll savor the shopping advice packed into each chapter.

- Sections on each component tell how it works—and how components work together.

- Software chapters reveal the computer's potential.

- **Bottom Line** buying tips quickly show differences and similarities, and why you'd care.

- **Jargon Busters** prepare you for the many hours you're sure to spend talking with computer dealers and mail-order staff.

- The many **Historical Figures** sections throughout this book provide fun ways to learn computing tidbits. When you finish the book, the **Glossary** serves as a ready refresher course.

- **Notes** reveal tips and techniques you'd otherwise need years to hit upon.

But What's the Right Way to Buy a Computer?

Which shopper is doing it the *right* way? Both. They're each gravitating toward the computer buying process that fits their time constraints and their personality.

Some people may think that researching and hunting down computer components and combining them into a computer set-up is a waste of time—especially if someone else (like the dealer) is willing to save them the trouble.

Other people enjoy the feeling that they've personally selected each component to fit their needs. Whatever shopping comfort-zone applies to you, you'll find this book addresses your needs.

Hey! I Don't Fit into Either Category!

A few of you may resent the idea of being pigeonholed into one shopper profile. You're right! Some people may have both tendencies.

Others move from one type to the other, over time. These shoppers may choose to buy a system package that's already configured, but then select a different monitor and video card. They might opt for a larger, faster hard disk. If that's you (it's me, too), this book can be a guide to only those components you want to explore further.

Whatever type of shopper you may be, you're human. And I've noticed a definite human tendency for people to want better and faster machines. With that in mind, each chapter contains information on upgrade paths.

All I Know Is, I Need Some Help!

Perhaps you're buying a computer for yourself or for a business. You may be helping someone else decide on a system. Whatever your situation, you picked up this book because you sensed you needed a guide to this perplexing process.

Buying a computer isn't easy. But this book can diminish confusion by keeping you organized, no matter how you actually shop.

How to Use This Book

Each chapter starts with a recap of topics covered in preceding chapters. This gives you a sense of how your knowledge is building, if you're the type that reads a book from cover to cover. If you're jumping around the different sections, the recap clues you into topics you've missed, so you can return later.

Chapters conclude with a summary of what you've learned, followed by questions to ask while out shopping.

Once inside the book, you can read it from front to back, or choose to skip some chapters and read only what concerns you at the moment. Either way, you'll find that each chapter is designed to break down part of a computer ad, identifying key terms and explaining components and their uses.

- If a salesperson or an ad tosses jargon at you, **Jargon Busters** helps you fight back by being familiar with key terms and their synonyms.

- **The Bottom Line** buying tips sprinkled throughout help you compare components and spot the best buy for your money.

- **Historical Figures** here and there provide some background—a Mr. Wizard session, if you will—for concepts that have always left you wondering "How in the world did they come up with *that*?"

- Plus, neat **Notes** give you additional information on the topics at hand.

- Key **Don't Forget to Ask** points keep you sharp while shopping.

When you're ready to buy, chapter checklists help you complete the Master Checklist found at the end of the book. Tear it out and take it with you. You're guaranteed to get the PC system you want.

So, What Are We Waiting for?!

Despite its good intentions, this book can't help you a bit unless you crack it open and use the many tools inside. So, why delay any longer? Turn to Chapter 1 and start getting the most PC for your money.

Acknowledgments

I'd like to thank Stephen Poland, Faithe Wempen, Linda Hawkins, and San Dee Phillips of Prentice Hall Computer Publishing for being pleasant, helpful, and full of good ideas. Special thanks also goes to Andrew Kleske, who put on his special jargon-filter cap.

Last, but not least, a big thank-you to my husband Andy, who took time out from his own book project to give guidance and encouragement.

Part I: "Er, Just Browsing"

Maybe you haven't yet experienced the pleasure of walking into a computer store. Or maybe one day you accidentally found yourself inside one—and scrammed out of there as fast as your high-tops could take you.

This section documents the fate of Bob Bungle—a guy who thought he could walk right into a computer store and buy a PC without doing any research whatsoever. (You can cover your eyes during the scary parts.)

Things get even hairier: Bernice, Bob's sister, is living proof that mail-order buying with no advance preparation poses just as many pitfalls to the unwary. (She lived to tell about it.)

Part One has a happy ending: at least for *you*. You'll see the right way to enter a computer store or shop by mail. Plus, you'll learn the steps involved in buying a PC. Best of all, you'll come to agree that even the teeniest burp of energy you put into researching your PC purchase will pay off in the end.

Computer Stores in Store for You

How *Not* to Enter a Computer Store

"You know, it's really time the Bungle family entered the Computer Age," Bob Bungle announced one Saturday morning. He glanced around the breakfast table for his family's reaction.

"Huh?" replied Penny, his wife. "Pass the Pop Tarts. Besides, we don't have anywhere to put a computer." Penny looked straight at Bob. "And don't even think about taking my woodworking room," she warned, referring to the corner of the den filled with refinishing projects.

"But, Dad, what do we need a computer for, anyway?" puzzled Marsha, age 11. Marsha's idea of fun was a romp through the nearby vacant fields with Hugo, the family spaniel, hunting down new beetles for her insect collection.

"Neat! Now I can have the gang over for Arkanoid," cheered Steve. The 13-year-old was a regular at the neighborhood arcade. "Think of all the quarters I can save," he crowed.

Despite the lukewarm response from everybody but Steve (and presumably Hugo, who was too busy nuzzling the empty Pop Tarts box to fully attend to the conversation), Bob Bungle was set on buying a computer. "Never put off 'til tomorrow what you can do today" was his motto.

If only he knew of a good computer store, Bob mused, as he slopped milk on his Nutty Loops. Suddenly a name popped into his brain— Mark! Mark from work would know. Not only did Mark own a home PC, but he'd mastered it to the point where folks at work turned to him with their computer questions. Bob resolved to phone his buddy Mark pronto.

"Mark, Bob Bungle here," Bob boomed into the phone. "Say, it's time the old Bungle family took the PC plunge. Where'd you buy your computer?" Bob lost no time getting to the point.

"Uh, Hi, Bob," Mark replied, cautiously. Mark could sense that Bob was in another one of his slapdash moods, which usually meant trouble for all concerned. "Sure, Bob. I can tell you where I bought my system," he began. "But you still need to research the best buy based on what you're going to do with your computer. Then you've got to do some comparison shopping."

"All that's for wimps," scoffed Bob. "Just tell me what store to hit, and I'll be back setting up my new system by afternoon."

"Have you thought of where you're going to put it?" Mark queried. "Remember, to be fully used by your whole family, the computer nook needs the right lighting, a degree of privacy, and a measure of accessibility. . . ."

"Oh, who cares about all that stuff!" Bob huffed, interrupting his friend. "Look, I'll talk to you later. Right now, I'm going shopping, even if I have to run over to the first place I see in today's paper." Bob hung up.

Grabbing the newspaper's business section, Bob Bungle spotted an ad for a nearby computer store. As he scanned for the store's address, he noticed the ad was packed with numbers and unfamiliar terms; it looked as if it were written in a foreign language. He buried the thought and headed for his car.

"Besides, I know a thing or two about computers from using one at work," Bob told himself reassuringly.

You Are Here

Bob Bungle circled the crowded parking lot for the second time. After fighting the urge to abandon his car on the sidewalk in front, he dashed through the bustling doors of Can-Do Computers.

As he stood in the doorway, slack-jawed at the sheer number of electronic doodads piled up everywhere, it occurred to Bob that he had no clue what half the gizmos did.

Staring as if he'd landed on a distant planet, Bob made his way down the packed aisles. Everywhere, small groups of shoppers conversed convincingly about the doodads—asking well-timed and intelligent-sounding questions of the sales staff.

The only words he recognized were names of numerals . . . so Bob vowed to keep a low profile for a while and "just look."

Studied Chaos

He meandered up and down the store's aisles, all the while feeling that the sales staff were watching him from behind the inventory piled in all those cardboard boxes everywhere. (Could the blank look on his face have anything to do with the fact that no one seemed eager to help him?)

Bob decided it must be his knowledgeable bearing that kept sales-people from approaching. "Boy, this buying a computer stuff is easy!" he chortled to himself. But soon enough, the novelty wore off. After another hour of aimless wandering—reading labels and staring at gadgets—Bob lost interest. He decided to search for a computer store with a personal touch.

Ahem. Do You Have an Appointment?

The salesman watched as Bob padded across the plush carpeting of Larchmont & Ritz Computers, Esq. Some fancy place, Bob thought, as he picked up a laptop and shook it.

"That's no Etch-A-Sketch, sir," glared the lone salesman. "Is there something we can help you with today? Hmmmm?"

"Yeah, uh, Yes. I guess I'm here to buy a computer," Bob stammered.

"Well, fill out this form, precisely stating your software's requirements, the peripherals you need, and your budgetary limitations, if you *have* any," the salesman intoned disdainfully, handing Bob a thick sheaf of papers, "and we'll make an appointment for, say, three weeks from today?"

Bob took the papers and, after a minute of examination, discovered he didn't understand one word. A prickly feeling started up his neck.

"I, I'll fill these out at home," said Bob, bounding for the door. He gave one sheepish glance backward as he opened the door, just in time to see the salesman roll his eyes.

The Aisle of the Swirling Monitors

Bob felt a surge of relief as he pulled into the now-familiar Can-Do Computers parking lot. Once inside he found himself drawn toward the bright displays flashing on a bank of computer screens.

Ah, here's something I can relate to, Bob thought. These light shows are cool. Neat! That all-black PC's saying something, almost like a TV commercial. . . . A host of images and colors soothed that uncomfortable, unprepared feeling that had plagued Bob all day.

Do They Always Talk in Numbers?

Heads up, Bob told himself as a saleswoman approached.

"I see you've found our top display," she started. "It's running SVGA with 1 meg of VRAM—at 1,024 by 768 with 256 colors and refresh rates of 72 hertz, it's state-of-the-art. It sports the new RAMDAC video chip, and its 16-inches does Windows just dandy. The one next to it offers local bus plus an 8514 card for the low, low price of only $1,500."

Bob had never heard anyone in this country speak that rapidly. Then again, maybe talking fast is easy when it's all numbers. As the saleswoman blazed on, Bob looked down at his shoes. That seemed to slow her down a bit. Then she paused. He made the fatal mistake of looking her in the eyes and nodding, which set her off again, at probably double her previous rate of speech.

Uh, I'll Take That One There

Suddenly Bob hit on a brilliant idea. If he took the top-of-the-line model, the saleswoman would think he knew what he was doing.

Bob and the saleswoman darted around the store, she firing descriptions at him and he motioning her to drop the items in his cart.

Home Sweet Home

Back home, with all the PC's boxes unloaded and piled up in the middle of the living room, Bob saw with mounting frustration that he might need Mark's help after all, at least to assemble the system, if not to explain what the darn thing did. If only Bob could think of a place to put it. . . .

And Now, the Right Way to Buy a Computer

Despite the warning signs every step of the way, Bob Bungle went about his computer purchase all backwards. Sure, he saved a few minutes of soul-searching and the trouble of doing some research, but he spent tons of money, he still doesn't really know why he wants a computer, and he certainly doesn't know what to do with what he bought.

Determine What You Want the Computer to Do

First, the Bungle family should have brainstormed ways they could use a new computer. A computer runs programs, often called *software*. Well, software exists for almost any purpose imaginable.

With the right software, Penny could have designed woodworking projects and kept records of materials, costs, and new sources. Beetle-fan Marsha could have cataloged her entire insect collection on the family PC.

We already know that Steve welcomed the chance to play video games on a home computer, but a little discussion could have sparked even better ways Steve could put one to use. Word processing software could help both kids complete homework assignments. And even Bob Bungle might have found a valid reason to own a computer—perhaps to organize his slapdash ways with a personal information manager software program!

Find the Software That Does the Job

Once the Bungles determined what they needed the computer to do, they should have found software that accomplished these goals. They could even see how they liked the software, by trying it out at computer stores, computer user groups, or perhaps, Mark's house.

Find the Best Hardware to Run the Software

Software packages list, right on the side of the box, what computer equipment, or *hardware*, they need to work properly. Once the Bungles decided on software they liked, one look at the box would tell them what type of hardware they should be considering.

Next, the family could have visited computer stores, comparing features and weighing performance against cost. After factoring in support and warranties, the Bungles could, with confidence, buy the Bungle-perfect system.

You don't have to be a computer greenhorn like Mr. Bungle. Armed with the sage advice this book offers, you'll undergo an enriching, enjoyable computer shopping experience.

Sizing Up a Computer Store

For every type of shopper there's a different type of computer store—each with its pros and cons. Use this section to evaluate the stores you encounter.

National Retail Chains

With names like Businessland and ComputerLand, and locations throughout the United States, these national chains compete heavily for your computer dollar. They carry name-brand, nationally recognized PCs, sometimes referred to as *IBM compatibles*.

Negotiate the price at these stores, and don't be afraid to use written quotes from other dealers as

Buy with a credit card whenever possible. Buyer protection, extended warranty, and even damage insurance give you a consumer's edge. Check with your card's bank to find out what consumer benefits they provide.

BOTTOM LINE

leverage. Investigate on-site repair facilities, after-sales support and warranties, including 30-day money-back guarantees, often used to jack up prices. Shopping for a PC you saw in an ad? Be sure to specify each component you want, to guarantee it's the identical system.

Local Clone Sellers

A *clone PC* is compatible with the IBM/PC standard, yet has a lesser-known or unknown brand name. Local clone dealers may have one or two stores in a city, or in a region. Their PCs are assembled on-site from inexpensive or commodity components. The result? Low prices and, usually, fairly decent systems. To keep inventory down and cash flow up, local clone dealers may build a system only after you order it.

A little research and homework into why systems and components differ will pay off if you decide to buy a computer this way.

In general, it's good to shop dealers as carefully as you shop PCs. Check any store's reputation with the local Better Business Bureau, local user groups, and computer societies.

Local clone dealerships should offer dealer-supported, one-year parts and labor warranties; on-site service; and after-sales support that extends to "free" classes. (*Nothing* is *free.*)

Josephine's Kustom Klones

Individuals who build custom-configured, "homebrewed" systems will make you a system to order. Locate these "brewers" through user groups, local computer publications, and computer fairs. In general, it's best to leave this buyer channel to those shoppers who know what they want—and how to tell whether they got it.

Because my philosophy is to teach you enough in this book so that you can shop even from a brewer, some guidelines apply if you choose this route:

First, read every chapter in this book and visit computer stores to examine components. Get a price quote in writing. Check to make sure this price beats local clone dealerships and mail-order vendors. Ask about on-site service. Look inside the PC's case; get each component brand, speed, capacity, and so on in writing.

Make sure the brewer services the warranty, and negotiate for a two-year parts/labor warranty. When the system's ready, ask the brewer to sit down with you and run a diagnostic software program like Norton's

System Information program. Diagnostic programs examine a PC and list its specific parts, speed, and so on, right on the screen.

Computer Superstores

High-volume sales ensure low prices. Still, it's worth a try to negotiate a price reduction on the brand-name PCs these huge national chains typically stock. Selection is great here—especially on extras like books and cables.

Membership Warehouse Stores

Stores such as Price Club or Office Club may not offer as wide a selection as stores dedicated only to selling computers. **Pluses:** Prices are among the lowest anywhere, and these stores carry nationally recognized brands. Some Price Club stores offer Tech Centers where trained staff help you select a system. Salespeople staffing warehouse stores' electronics departments might not be knowledgeable on the very latest products, although stores differ widely. Ask for details on the type of support a membership warehouse offers.

The Appliance Store

Selection can be sparse. Besides, will you be buying a computer from someone who sells vacuum cleaners for a living? Just who will repair the computer if it breaks down?

The University Bookstore's Computer Corner

Courteous and knowledgeable salespeople who take time to listen to your needs count here. If you're a student, find out what discounts you can negotiate (these can be sizable). Name-brand systems are the rule. Check for details on repair, warranty, and support.

In This Chapter, You Learned . . .

The misadventures of Bob Bungle showed you how *not* to buy a computer. Buying one the right way is easy if you follow these steps:

- **First:** Decide what you need a computer for.

- **Second:** Find the software to accomplish those tasks.

- **Third:** Track down a software package you like, and see what type of hardware it needs to run best.

- **Fourth:** Price and compare similar hardware components and PC systems, as well as warranties, support, free classes, and so on.

- **Fifth:** Buy the best PC system you can afford.

Chapter 1 Checklist: Assessing a Computer Store

- Approved by the Better Business Bureau?
- Liberal return policy?
- On-site repair facilities?
- Dealer will deal or, at least, will throw in extras like software, extended support/warranty, and so on?
- Dealer installs and configures PC?

Don't Forget to Ask . . .

- What does the warranty include? Parts and labor? No questions asked?
- Should you choose to return it, will there be a restocking fee?
- How long has the company been in business?

Notes: _____

_____

_____

_____

Notes: _____

_____

_____

_____

_____

_____

_____

_____

_____

_____

_____

_____

_____

_____

_____

_____

_____

Mail-Order Shopping for a Computer

Chapter 1 showed you how to (and how not to) shop in computer stores. In this chapter, you'll learn about another way to shop that's far from foolproof.

Mail-Order Maladroit

Bernice Bungle put down the letter from her brother, Bob. Sheesh! What a mess he'd gotten himself into when he bought a personal computer! She almost laughed out loud when she thought of all the times Bob's hasty, slapdash nature had gotten him into hot water as a kid.

Bernice wanted a PC, too—something to help her run her small retail outlet, Bernice's Beauty Barn. She knew that her rival across town, Eunice Euler, used a computer at her place, Eunice's Elegance Emporium. Hah, the nerve! Bernice bristled. (The very name *Eunice* sent Bernice into fits.)

To be sure, Bernice wasn't quite clear about what her competitor *did* with the machine. No matter. Bernice wasn't about to watch Eunice and her high-tech contraption corner the beauty-supplies market in their town.

Why Not Buy Mail-Order?

Bernice decided that buying a computer mail-order was the way to go. Rather, Cousin Louie decided for her. Years ago, Louie bought his computer through the mail, and he never let anyone forget what a great deal he got. If mail-order computers were good enough for Louie, they were good enough for Bernice, she reasoned.

Just Look at That One!

Dragging a stack of computer magazines home one afternoon, Bernice could hardly contain her excitement. Everything looked so good. Once in a while, she'd come across articles offering advice on how to buy a particular component, but they looked too dull.

Bernice decided to skip the articles, opting instead to look at the pictures in the ads. Besides, who has time to read, these days? There she'd be, holed up reading computer articles, and meanwhile, Eunice would be grabbing up all her hard-won business.

Just then, Bernice Bungle landed on a page that really caught her eye. That's the computer for me!, Bernice told herself. A real bargain, to boot. She dialed the ad's phone number, credit card in hand.

A pleasant salesman answered the phone. After a short talk (with him doing all the talking), Bernice headed over to her bank to buy some cashier's checks. The nice young man on the phone said that was the best way to pay for her new computer system—the one that would really put Eunice in a snit.

"For Technical Support, Please Hold . . . "

It's probably just a minor glitch, Bernice thought, as she navigated the computer company's voice mail. She'd had her computer only three weeks—a week and a half just getting the neighbor kid to set it up— and already it didn't work right.

Funny how I didn't have to hold this long when I called to order the darn thing, Bernice fumed under her breath. The recorded voice droned on about which extensions to press.

After two days of fruitless phoning, Bernice fired off a complaint letter. A week later, the mailbox held a familiar looking envelope, marked "Company Moved, No Forwarding Address."

And Now, the Right Way to Buy Mail-Order

Bernice Bungle ended up with a fancy doorstop and (hopefully) a lesson learned. It didn't have to be that way.

If only Bernice had thought a little about what she needed the computer to do, she could have researched software, compared hardware, and phoned a few vendors to assess their reliability, purchase policy, and support.

Poor Bernice. At least she and brother Bob will have something to talk about at family reunions.

Reputation Comes First

Hunt down local computer groups, often called *user groups,* and attend one of their meetings. Ask members to relate all mail-order experiences, good and bad. Take notes.

Call the mail-order vendors that interest you, and ask how long they've been in business. Have them send you a brochure or price list with their sales and support policies in writing.

> *Buying a computer through the mail is one of the most expensive and complex transactions you'll ever make. Satisfy yourself about the vendor's reputation and reliability. Check with the Better Business Bureau in the vendor's city. Call the Direct Marketing Association (212-768-7277) to see how the vendor rates with them.*

BOTTOM LINE

You might try calling the vendors and asking outright for (recent) customer references. This may seem outlandishly bold. On the other hand, computer vendors are a competitive breed, and they want your business.

Courtesy Pays

Call a few vendors and discuss the system you have in mind. Use these preliminary conversations to assess the sales staff for important qualities such as knowledgeability, friendliness, willingness to take time for you, and skill in communicating. These qualities will blow up to gargantuan proportions once you buy a system.

Sales and Service Policies Count

Accept nothing less than a 30-day, unquestioned, money-back guarantee. Many mail-order dealers charge a *restocking fee* for returned merchandise. Ask first, but don't agree to such a fee, especially if you return the PC in new condition. And find out who pays shipping costs. You shouldn't. Even for returns.

Warranties and Repairs

What's their repair policy? If an electrical component is going to fail, it's usually within the first 30 days. Insist on a one-year parts-and-labor warranty, at least. Some vendors offer two-year warranties, although the extended version might include either parts or labor—usually not both. Try to negotiate a two-year parts-and-labor warranty when you're dealing.

Ask who will honor the warranty. Make sure it's the dealer—not the manufacturer. Typical PC systems contain components made by many different manufacturers—a monitor from one, a hard disk drive from another. Imagine having to keep track of phone numbers, addresses, shipping records, and technical support for each one!

If you find a problem with your new system, whose dime do you spend to call technical support? Make sure tech support keeps accessible hours, preferably some periods on weekends or during evenings. Obtain a toll-free number.

Make sure the mail-order company has on-site repair facilities—that's where the repairperson comes right to your house. You don't want your PC enduring any more shipping than is absolutely necessary. And insist on reasonable turnaround time on repairs.

Ask About Bulletin-Board Support

Perhaps the mail-order company offers customer support on a computer *bulletin board system*, often called a *BBS*. If so, the company runs special *bulletin board* software on a dedicated computer that's connected at all times to a phone line. Computer bulletin boards give a company an easy way to distribute information, helpful programs, and news to customers.

Here's how it works, in brief. (For detailed information about bulletin boards and other computer communications, check out Chapter 19.) You dial the phone number of the bulletin board computer using a special device known as a *modem*, which connects to your computer and to an ordinary phone line. Give two computers each a modem and they can talk to each other. The modems break down the computers' digital instructions into signals that can travel over phone lines and then put the signals back into computer-readable shape at the other end.

Your computer can connect to the bulletin board computer anytime it's receiving calls, no matter how distant the mail-order company's location. Once you're connected, you can navigate the company's

Jär-gen:

The electronic bulletin board is similar in concept to a physical bulletin board at work or in a supermarket, where people post notices, classified ads, lost-and-found advisories, and other informative stuff. But computer bulletin boards allow electronic information exchange, over ordinary phone lines.

bulletin board computer as if it were your own. You can dig up special software and read customer comments and informational bulletins. You can even *download* (bring into your own computer) utility software that the manufacturer wrote to make your computer run better.

Merchandise Ready to Ship

When ordering a computer through the mail, nail down a firm ship date. Make sure the merchandise is ready to ship soon after you place your order.

Pay with a Credit Card

At some point in the shopping process, you may be offered a discount if you pay cash. Don't do it. Buying with a credit card means your bank card company will back you up in case of a dispute or, worse, a no-show. Credit card purchases guarantee many other consumer rights. Check with your credit card bank to see just what you're getting for that annual fee you pay for your credit card.

Make sure the vendor charges your account only after the system is actually shipped. Determine how billing takes place in advance so there won't be any surprises.

Refuse to Pay Extra for Credit Card Purchases

Some mail-order houses try to tack on an extra fee for credit card purchases, typically 3 to 7 percent. If this happens to you, report it immediately to your credit card company. Depending on what card you use, you may not have to pay the surcharge.

American Express is one company that allows surcharges. Most don't. Check with your bank card for their policy.

In This Chapter, You Learned . . .

Mail-order shopping can be a convenient cost cutter, but only if you check out the seller in advance and get the facts straight while you're buying.

Make notes of all telephone conversations, and be sure to get the names of all employees you talk to.

Finally, pay by credit card, if at all possible. You can still pay off your purchase at the end of the month, but you'll be protected with the consumer coverage many cards (check with your company before you assume any coverage) provide.

Jär-gen:

Acceptance   The maximum amount of time you have to decide whether a purchase is acceptable (seller can limit this if you agree to it).

FOB, short for Free On Board   Determines if dealer's jurisdiction over a shipment ends when product leaves dealer or remains in effect until shipment arrives to you.

Prices Subject to Change   Seller may reserve the right to switch prices on you.

Chapter 2 Checklist:
Assessing a Mail-Order House

- At least a 30-day, no-questions-asked, money-back return policy?

- No restocking fee should I choose to return the PC?

- Merchandise in stock, ready to ship?

- No fee for paying by credit card?

- Credit card debited when order ships, not before?

- One-year warranty on parts and labor? Ask them to extend that to two years.

- Dealer warranty instead of manufacturer warranty?

- Accessible telephone tech-support, toll-free?

- Polite, patient, and knowledgeable sales and support staff?

- Service takes place on-site, avoiding additional shipping?

- Reasonable turnaround time on repairs/replacements?
- Electronic BBS (Bulletin Board System) support for customers with modems?

Notes: _____

_____

_____

_____

_____

_____

_____

_____

_____

_____

_____

_____

Notes: _____

_____

_____

_____

_____

_____

_____

_____

_____

_____

_____

_____

_____

_____

_____

_____

_____

_____

Part II: Sort Out Your Software Needs

The only reason for even going through this computer-buying stuff is so you can run some software. So, we'd look pretty silly ignoring the matter.

Here's where we sift through all the software on the shelves and find some packages that will make that lump of bits and bolts do something. (Your PC, that is; we can't do much about your car. . . .)

You'll cross your legs in a meditative pose (just pretend to do *this* part—so we don't incur any lawsuits), and you'll focus on the tasks you need to do. A peek into the computer rooms of some other people (we got their permission, first) will help you see what other users do with their systems. And then we'll get a close-up look at the different tasks you can do with a computer, and the software that does 'em.

What Do You Want to Do with Your Computer?

In Chapters 1 and 2, Bob and Bernice "bungled" their computer purchases by not taking the right steps. That won't happen to you. You're about to take the first step in buying a computer right now— thinking about the types of software you'll want to use on your new PC.

First, you'll list all the tasks you want your PC to help you accomplish. Then you'll read about six typical PC situations. You'll see the tasks these PC owners do each day. You'll learn the types of software they use, and you'll see why each user has chosen a particular PC to run that software.

By the time you leave this chapter, you'll have an idea of how you might use a PC. You may want to hang around for Chapter 4, where you'll find details on the different kinds of software, as well as what PCs run each software type best.

Sit Down, Take Your Shoes Off . . .

Find an easy chair and relax with a cool beverage. Grab a pen and some paper. This step doesn't involve driving anywhere or looking at complex equipment. Instead, sit back, breathe deeply a few times, and focus on you—and the tasks *you* need to accomplish.

*Many computer shoppers fail to enjoy their new systems because they neglected the one basic rule: **The only reason to buy computer hardware is to run software.** That's because it's software that actually performs the tasks. Without the instructions contained in software, computers would qualify for the paperweight-of-the-month club, and little more.*

Right now, don't worry about software, or anything else. Just list whatever tasks come to mind when you think of being productive with your new computer.

_____

_____

_____

_____

Now it's time to don your wizard's cap and grab your crystal ball. What do you see you and your computer accomplishing two years from now? Find your pencil (first throw down your crystal ball) and jot down as many ideas as you can.

_____

_____

_____

_____

Okay. Enough predictions for now. We'll use your task list throughout this book, so make sure the dog doesn't eat it (the list, not the book).

What's Software and Why Is It So Important?

Software is the cushion between you and the nuts-and-bolts machinery. It's the "personal" in personal computer. The only way to get a computer to do something is to load it with purchased, pre-packaged software. Software contains all the instructions to make a computer accomplish a particular task, like print a memo or simulate a game.

Software Is Like Music

People use lots of comparisons when they try to explain software. Perhaps the most useful one likens software to the audio cassette or CD you throw on your stereo system to get it to play music. A music publisher records an artist's music onto the cassette's magnetic tape and sells it in a music store. Well, a software publisher records a computer application onto a form of magnetic media known as a *diskette* and sells it in a software store.

A music lover buys a stereo system knowing it will play many different kinds of music: country, jazz, classical, and even Weird Al. Likewise, someone who buys a PC from the IBM-compatible family can look forward to "playing" hundreds of types of software: games, word processors, and even garden-design programs.

(Of course, a hard-core Weird Al fan might choose to listen to nothing else on his stereo; just as a dedicated doodler might use only a drawing program on her PC. These people are generally avoided at company picnics . . . .)

The similarities extend all the way to legal issues. When someone buys a tape, dubs it, and gives a copy to a friend, that person is breaking the music publisher's copyright and depriving the artist of royalties. When a person buys a software program and copies it onto diskettes for a friend, that person's breaking the same basic laws.

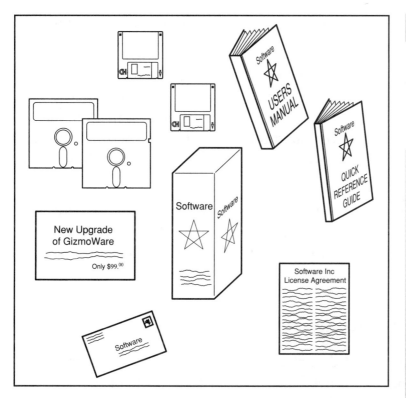

Figure 3.1

Contents of a typical software package.

Jär-gen:

Another name for software is application, because the software provides a way to apply the computer to a task. Sometimes you'll see app, for short. Software can be called a program, too, because the software is written (or programmed) with a special programming language. You'll see software package, too, because it usually comes in a shrink-wrapped package filled with diskettes, manuals, warranties, and even ads for other software, as in Figure 3.1.

Why Can't I Just Buy My Software After I Get My Computer, Like Everyone Else?

Not all software packages are created equal. PCs differ, too. Hoggish, complex programs strain even the biggest machine's capabilities. Other, more

Always buy a slightly larger system than your software requires, with an eye to the future.

BOTTOM LINE

elegant programs hardly consume any computer resources.

Big or small, each software program has minimal hardware requirements in order to run properly. Since these requirements are listed on the software's box, once you know what software you want to use, you'll know the minimum-strength PC to buy, as shown in Figure 3.2.

The kinds of software you'll load onto your new computer determine whether you need a color monitor, how much hard disk space you need, how fast the computer runs, how much expansion room you'll need, and even the type of printer you should buy.

Six System Scenarios

The following situations describe different, typical PC user scenarios. You may find your needs overlapping into two or more of these examples. Even better. Just don't forget to jot down all the other tasks you find to do on your new computer.

For more details on the software mentioned in the examples, scurry over to Chapter 4.

Figure 3.2

Software requirements listed on the package help you run the program under the most satisfactory hardware conditions.

I Want to Bring Work Home from the Office

Ed's an accountant. At work, he runs a spreadsheet program that calculates his company's financial status. Since large spreadsheets tax the average computer with heavy numeric calculations, Ed uses a fast

486 computer. Ed bought a similar PC for home, where he's running a purchased copy of his spreadsheet software.

The software runs under a program called Microsoft Windows, so Ed bought a copy of that, too. The Windows program works by letting users point at pictures (*icons*) on the screen, instead of typing commands with a keyboard. The pointing device, known as a *mouse* (Chapter 15), eases spreadsheet work on Ed's home computer setup.

Ed may want to buy a *modem* that works with communications software to send computer data over the phone line to another computer. This way he could *telecommute*, sending completed work to his office computer without leaving his den.

We Need a Family Computer for Writing, Educational Programs, and Organizing Stuff

Specialized database software helps the Trujillos keep track of their huge record collection, as well as their prized recipes. They use a low-priced word processor to write letters to Grandma. The kids enjoy playing math arcade games that boost their test scores while improving hand/eye coordination.

One of the most useful additions to the family's software arsenal was an inexpensive home printing program called The Print Shop. It's designed to be easy for kids to use, but all the family find themselves creating simple greeting cards, stationery, banners, and invitations with this program and their inexpensive, 9-pin dot-matrix printer.

The family is interested in an *on-line service* they've seen advertised, called Prodigy. Prodigy, and services like it, enable families to meet and to share interests with other families, via modem, across the nation. The Trujillos will need a modem to use Prodigy; they'll also pay a $13 monthly fee. If they do buy a modem, they're planning to investigate a software program called CheckFree, which will let them pay their bills electronically.

The family manages with a 386SX computer equipped with a fairly small hard disk to store programs on, and an inexpensive dot-matrix printer that can print nice-looking letters.

I'm a College Student and Need a Computer for Schoolwork

Whatever major Mary chooses, she figures she'll always have a term paper due. Unfortunately, Mary is short on cash, and can't spend a lot on a fancy computer. She bought a word processing program, and she uses a personal finance program to keep track of tuition hikes. She's thinking of hooking up her black-and-white monitor and low-cost 286 PC with a modem to run communications software. That way she can grab term-paper fodder from research databases, and even access the library's card catalog.

Because a modem works with the ordinary phone line in her off-campus apartment, Mary must choose her modeming sessions carefully so she won't tie up the phone when her roommates need to use it.

A Computer Could Help Us with Our Small Business

Writing business letters and invoices, spitting out mailing labels and memos: the high-end word processing software works almost as hard as Carl and Susan to keep their small business afloat.

The partners use an *integrated* software package to cover their other computing needs. Integrated software offers several different modules rolled into one, low-cost package, as Figure 3.3 shows. It runs great on their low-priced 386SX computer. Carl and Susan use its spreadsheet for finances, its database for client records, and the communications module with their modem to converse with other users on small-business-oriented computer bulletin boards.

Small businesses should buy a larger system than they need, or an upgradable system, in case the business expands. Never fear success!

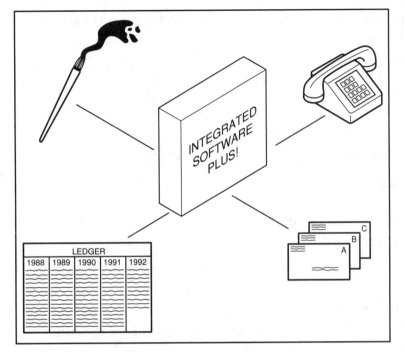

Figure 3.3

Integrated software combines useful programs that accomplish many tasks.

I'm a Graphics Designer and I Want to Do Desktop Publishing

Leah and Kay run a custom publishing business that provides graphic design and layout services for their clients. Their complex desktop publishing software demands a fast 486 computer with the capacity to store lots of software and data, plus a mouse to highlight text and manipulate page design.

A large, two-page display monitor with excellent resolution helps, too. A sharp laser printer helps them design effective layouts. A device called a *scanner* lets them transform ordinary photographic slides into computer graphics, ready to be inserted into documents.

They use a modem, too, to send files to service bureaus for processing. All of their programs run under the graphic user software Microsoft Windows. They also use a contact-management software program that helps them prospect for new clients.

Our Whole Family's Addicted to Computer Games— We Need One with the Works!

The entire Chou family enjoys sessions with their state-of-the-art computer golf game. Arcade games attract the more agile family members, and adventure games with movie-quality color and sound are popular, too. That's why they invested in a powerful 486 PC with a large hard disk.

They bought an oversized color monitor and a video card capable of showing hundreds of colors at once. A sound card and stereo speakers add realism by letting them hear the many digitized voices, musical scores, and sound effects incorporated into today's games. Their computer is equipped with a joystick, similar to the controller in an arcade game, which lets them dodge spacecraft and blast the bad guys without using the clunky keyboard.

The Chous recently bought an electronic music keyboard that attaches to their PC. They use it with their sound card and music-composing software to write their own songs. What fun! Next on the family's list is animation software that will let them create and play back their own movies.

HISTORY

Music: The Universal Language

Believe it or not, a music program has bragging rights to being the first *monitor* on the very first personal computer.

The computer, the Altair 8800, also discussed in Chapter 5, came in one of those kits that electronics enthusiasts were always building (back in the days before they all became computer nerds!). The trouble was, it had no keyboard, and certainly no mouse. The only way you could get information into the thing was by force-feeding arcane commands by way of tiny switches along the machine's front.

Worse yet, the Altair had no monitor, or even a speaker. The only way you could get information out of the thing was to read bizarre

continues

continued

code in the base 8 number system off a tiny, flashing LED light. Then you had to translate that into decimal, or base 10, numbers!

All this changed the day a guy left his radio on while working with his Altair one night. He was surprised to hear the radio wail after he'd pushed the computer's run button. One more try yielded the same, baffling results. It seems that the radio frequency interference resulted from the bits switching around inside the Altair.

A light came on in the guy's head. If he sat down with his electric guitar and mapped out all the sounds, he could figure out the computer memory locations of all the notes and write a music program. At the next meeting of the Homebrew Computer Club, the proud Altair owner set his computer down and set it up to sputter the notes to "Fool on the Hill." The crowd cheered: the tinny little tune confirmed their dreams of a home computer that could do something.

In This Chapter, You Learned . . .

The only reason to buy a computer is to run software. Software gives instructions that tell the computer to perform a particular task. Since software varies in its hardware requirements, in order to buy the best

PC for your money, it's important for you to define your needs and to think of what types of software will accomplish your goals.

This chapter shows that choosing a computer depends on assessing your computing situation. A look at the scenarios in the chapter can give you an idea of the often bewildering (but always exciting!) proliferation of computing choices that exist. Brainstorming some of your options will help prepare you for the shopping experience that awaits you.

Chapter 3 Checklist:

- How can I use a computer right now to accomplish my goals?
- What will I be doing with my computer in two years to accomplish my goals?
- What user scenarios can give me additional computing inspiration?

Notes: _____

_____

_____

_____

To Run This Software . . .

The first part of this book showed how crucial it is to take the right steps when buying a PC. In the last chapter, you saw why choosing software is the first step. Then you thought about possible software programs for your own computing situation.

Let's learn more about the various software packages: what they can do for you and what PC systems run them best.

Because you worked on your computer task list in Chapter 3, it only makes sense to organize this chapter by task. Skim the headings; if you don't see a task you need to do, don't bother reading that section.

First, the Operating System

Software differs greatly from one package to the next. Some programs are deadeye straight and serious. Others are whimsical and madcap. Because they vary, programs can't be installed directly onto a computer. The computer hardware could never anticipate the many diverse, often quirky, ways each program chooses to talk to the rest of the PC.

Instead, software communicates with a special type of middleman software called an *operating system*, which then communicates to the

PC. The operating system (often shortened to *OS* and pronounced *oh-ess*) provides a way to organize files, to copy data to and from diskettes, and to perform other housekeeping tasks.

MS-DOS (pronounced *em-ess-doss* and often seen as just *DOS*) is the name of the operating system that runs on most PCs. It stands for Microsoft DOS, one brand that's available.

What If I Don't Want DOS?

No fair! You don't even get to choose it, as you do the other types of software. When you buy a computer, the dealer generally sets up DOS on your computer.

Make sure you've purchased a licensed copy and you get the full set of user manuals.

In fact, it's hard to tell if a computer's working right if DOS isn't there, as it goes through many self-testing routines when the computer's first turned on.

So, there MS-DOS sits on your PC's hardware, like the first layer of a chocolate cake sitting on a platter. When you buy a "real" software package, you'll install it right on top of DOS. This software is the cake's second layer. (Yum.) After you're finished using your software program and tell it you're ready to quit—Boom, Thud—you're back to the bottom layer, DOS.

Once you're face-to-face with DOS (alone in a cheap hotel room, with only the blinking Eat at Joe's sign outside to relieve the oppressive darkness), you'll see why DOS is legendary for being difficult. In DOS, you type cryptic, short commands that hardly ever spell real words. Worse yet, you have to memorize these blurtings.

That's why another layer for the cake was invented: *Microsoft Windows.*

What Does Windows Need (and How Come It Needs So Much)?

Microsoft Windows isn't an operating system, technically, because it still needs MS-DOS to run underneath it. It's called an operating *environment.* Normal software-to-make-the-computer-do-something runs on top, making the Windows cake a three-layer extravaganza (yum).

If you choose to run it, Windows does away with complex, heartless DOS by coming in between DOS and you, the user. Windows lets you get things done by pointing to pictures (*icons*) with a mouse, instead of typing cryptic commands. Because it has pictures and it's an interface between you and DOS, Windows is known as a *GUI* (pronounced *gooey*), or *graphical user interface* (see Figure 4.1).

Figure 4.1

Windows' GUI lets you run programs in friendly, easy-to-use window panes.

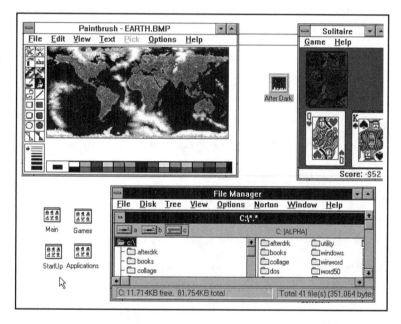

If Windows Makes Computing So Easy, Why Doesn't Everybody Use It?

Partly because it works with pictures instead of text commands, Windows and Windows-compatible software programs are generally large and quite demanding on a PC's hardware. Expect to pay more for your computer, monitor, and hard disk (even your printer, if you do it right) if you choose to run Windows the way it should be run.

Why Aren't There Other Operating Systems?

Plenty of other operating systems vie with each other for designation as bottom layer. UNIX, OS/2, and DR-DOS are some other IBM PC-compatible operating systems.

Not everyone can afford to run Windows and some prefer not to bother with Windows at all. Unless your software requires the Windows environment, you'd be better off without it, because some DOS programs don't run well under Windows.

BOTTOM LINE

Whatever operating system you run, your software programs must be compatible with that operating system. While you're looking at software, you might see a package that looks interesting, but it turns out to be *Macintosh-compatible.* That means it runs under the Macintosh operating system (which runs on a different type of personal computer), and you can't run it on your MS-DOS PC.

Here's another example. In the unlikely case that you wanted to run UNIX on your PC, and you liked the WordPerfect word processor, you'd need to buy WordPerfect for UNIX. (The DOS version of WordPerfect wouldn't find the bottom layer it was expecting, and it would sulk and refuse to operate.)

MS-DOS was the first operating system for IBM PC-compatibles. (*DOS* stands for Disk Operating System, by the way.) It's deeply entrenched in the PC marketplace, because most of the software for PCs is MS-DOS-compatible. And it's the one you'll probably start with (even stay with).

Ideal Computer Systems for . . .

Here comes the software! Search the following subheads for tasks on your list, and you'll find a description of additional tasks the software can do. You won't find recommendations on which software to buy, or lengthy descriptions on each software's features, because this book focuses on hardware shopping.

You can skim over the hardware suggestions in each section for now because many of the terms are still unfamiliar. Remember where to find them for later, though.

Newsletters, Articles, Books

If your tasks include writing business or personal letters; writing articles, books, or poetry; or doing minor page layout for simple newsletters or even business cards, you need a word processor. Word processors let you easily change a document, reformat it, even change the style of the lettering—without ever having to retype a draft or drag out the correction fluid. Some include grammar checkers to sharpen your pencil a bit; simple spelling checkers and a thesaurus are also features to look for.

Word processing software runs from simple to feature-laden and huge. The PC for a simple, no-frills word processing package might dip as low on the cost and performance scale as a 286 PC with a monochrome monitor and a 40MB hard drive. WordPerfect, a popular program, is shown in Figure 4.2.

If you plan to run the massive GUI programs such as Ami Pro, Word for Windows, or WordPerfect for Windows, buy at least a 386/33 with an 80MB hard disk and a VGA color monitor. A mouse is crucial for any Windows program. These high-flying word processors take full advantage of a laser printer.

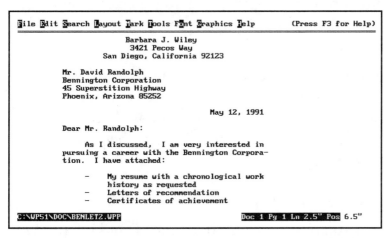

Figure 4.2

WordPerfect is the most popular word processing program.

Checkbooks and Business Data

If you plan to work with numbers, you'll want a spreadsheet software program. Spreadsheets work like a multiplication grid, only you can perform any operation (even complex scientific formulas) on a number.

Spreadsheet software programs are great fun for playing "what if": what type of mansion can you afford if you land that 25 percent raise and then interest rates fall 3 percent? Even if you don't need one for your primary tasks, they're essential for budgeting. High-priced packages, such as Excel, Lotus 1-2-3, and Quattro Pro for Windows, let you transform numbers from your spreadsheet to pie charts, bar charts, and so on—perfect for slide presentations. A sample spreadsheet and graph are shown in Figure 4.3.

Simple spreadsheets that you'll use only occasionally require a midrange PC such as a 386SX. Frequent spreadsheeters will want a more powerful computer, as will those who plan to use Excel or another spreadsheet that runs under Windows. A mouse helps to navigate a spreadsheet program.

Address Listings, Inventories, Client Data

Database software lets you organize collections and client lists; produce mailing labels and membership records; even track your garden seeds. A database arranges data of any kind. Think of a database as an electronic filing cabinet that sorts itself and retrieves information at the press of a button.

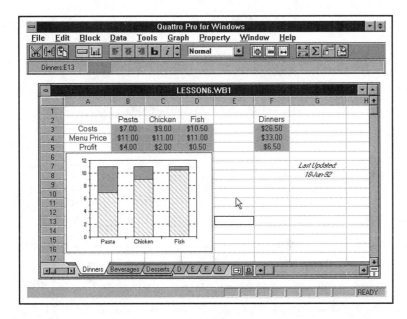

Figure 4.3

High-end spreadsheet programs let you create graphs.

Very simple databases look like index-card files and perform like electronic address books. (You'll never have to use correction fluid again for that friend who moves every year.)

More complex database software breaks down each *record* (index card) into *fields*—one field for last name, one for first name, one for street name, another field for ZIP code. After typing in data, you can sort fields in endless ways. You might produce a list of all your clients named Smith with Iowa ZIP codes who bought something from you in June, for example.

Just as with spreadsheets, occasional database users don't need beefed-up PCs. If large databases, or database programming, are in your plans, however, be sure to get a faster PC with lots of hard disk storage and plenty of memory: A fast 386 or even a 486 PC with at least 8MB of main memory and a 100MB hard disk would be about right.

Page Layout and Graphic Design

The many types of software in this category let you publish newsletters, design flyers, create computer art, or remodel a kitchen. Desktop publishing software provides the user with the ability to lay out documents without having to physically cut and paste pieces of paper. Graphics software arms the user with an electronic paintbrush and canvas. Computer-assisted design programs come with rooms already planned for you to modify. Some programs allow photo retouching and image reduction or reversal. This ever-changing field presents some of the most exciting uses for a PC.

Although low-end programs put less strain on a PC, the results from the cheaper programs might not be satisfactory for a professional. The high-end desktop publishing and graphics software are large and memory-hungry because just displaying a picture is hard work for a PC. A professional desktop publisher needs a fast PC with a large, two-page color monitor; a mouse, a hand-held or flatbed scanner; and a hefty hard drive. The truly serious professional would consider a tape-backup device for safekeeping large files, as well as a CD-ROM drive for accessing large collections of digitized pictures (also called *clip art*).

As you can see, desktop publishing and graphics are among the most hardware-intensive tasks a PC can accomplish.

Taxes, Education, Home Design, Writing

Designing a new deck, tracking tax deductions, writing the great American novel in your spare time: Household software can be any "business" software that's applied to home use.

A low-priced 386 computer with plenty of hard drive space, a color monitor, a mouse, and a joystick will see the family through many hours of rewarding PC time. Consider a sound card and some stereo speakers to enhance a home PC. If communicating with others over the computer seems like fun, you'll want to try out some communications software and buy a modem.

Writing Programs, Tinkering with Your Setup

If making a computer do your bidding sounds appealing, you'll enjoy computer programming. For that you'll need to buy one or more *programming languages* software packages, and teach yourself by writing small programs at first—then larger and more complex programs.

Utilities (another type of software) help your computer run better. If there's a lack or deficiency with PCs, someone out there has programmed a utility to fix it. These programs will optimize your hard drive, make your printer print sideways, check a diskette for viruses, or make your keyboard easier to use.

As with the other types of software, buying the best PC for programming and utilities software depends on the amount of time you'll devote to these pursuits. A midrange 386SX might be a good place to start. You can migrate to a bigger system in a few years if you find yourself writing huge programs or running large utility software packages. (Or writing large utility packages—utilities are among the first programs programmers write.)

Playing Games and Making Music

Computer games abound; if you get even the slightest pleasure from cards, board games, video arcades, or mystery novels, there's a computer game somewhere for you. As with the other types of software, games range from simple and undemanding to huge, colorful, expensive, and PC-intensive. Read the individual packages to be sure of the requirements.

NOTE

Although it may seem foolish to invest money in a home computer dedicated solely to gaming and music, your home PC can be the source of ongoing, rewarding family fun. Computers are much more stimulating and interactive than television.

Many of the high-end games take full advantage of sound cards. Some games offer sophisticated synthesizer scores throughout their duration, as if you were "playing" a computerized movie. Once you have a sound card, you can write and play music if you invest in an electronic keyboard and a music program.

Where to Learn More About Software

Read computer magazines to learn about other types of software you might want to use. These magazines run articles about new products and offer detailed software comparisons that are written by experienced users. Look for ads that offer demo programs. Send away for these, even if you have to try them out on a friend's computer.

Visit software stores and get in the habit of reading a software box for its system requirements. Ask if you can try out a package (most stores will be happy to oblige).

Plan on at least one session at a computer *user group*, where people with similar PC interests gather monthly and exchange ideas, tips, and even horror stories. Try out more software here. Ask questions and ask those who share your software interests what type of PC they own.

Don't forget your friends. Grill them about their software experiences. Sit down at their PCs and check out the software they like. Ask what makes their favorite software better than the others. (People love showing off their PCs.)

Shareware: A Different Way to Buy Software

Some software publishers make their software available on a try-before-you-buy basis. This software is called *shareware* because it can be passed around (or *shared*) for free, unlike commercial software.

You pay for a shareware program when you find yourself using it regularly and enjoying it. Then you're on your honor to send a fee (usually lower than what you'd pay for commercial software) to the program's author. User groups and electronic bulletin boards are great sources for shareware. The one drawback to shareware is that, because it travels around to so many PCs, you must screen it for *viruses*— destructive programs written by bad people—using a special anti-virus utility program.

In This Chapter, You Learned . . .

The only way to accomplish your goals with a PC is to find software designed for those goals. Within each software category, you'll find a range of programs that perform both simple and complex tasks. The more complex a program is, the more strain it puts on the PC hardware. Because software packages vary so, software boxes list their program's hardware requirements.

Before you buy a PC, determine the tasks a software package can do, and then look at the software's box to get a rough idea of the PC system you'll need for it. To narrow down your software choices, read reviews, try out software at stores, and visit user groups. Try out your friends' software, too. Shareware's a great resource if you're cautious.

Chapter 4 Checklist:

My task list requires the following software types:

_____

_____

_____

The packages I like so far require the following:

DOS version: _____

Memory: _____

Video display: _____

Printer: _____

Mouse: _____

Hard disk space: _____

Notes: _____

_____

_____

_____

_____

_____

_____

_____

_____

_____

_____

_____

Notes: _____

_____

_____

_____

_____

_____

_____

_____

_____

_____

_____

_____

_____

_____

_____

_____

Part III: (Finally) Inside the PC

Isn't it about time we quit digging our toe into the sand and stepped up to home plate, bat in hand, ready to hit a homer? (Or we *could* just drive to the computer store. . . .)

Let's pry the case off one of these suckers and see what's inside.

Just remember to let the nice clerk in the store do all the digging around in there for you, or you'll be besieged with hordes of customers asking you questions with lots of long numbers in them.

The Processor Process

In Chapter 4, you found out that software, like a small child, will make you aware of its needs (although it won't tug at your trousers). You skimmed the main types of software, with stuffy names like word processors and spreadsheets, and you learned the ideal computer system to run each kind happily. Wisely, you didn't focus too much on the systems' specifics right then, instead saving the whole discussion in the secret now-I-know-for-later area of your brain.

Even so, you probably discovered a pattern in the system descriptions. They all had numbers that ended in 86—such as 386, 486, and so on. (Could it be? Order and consistency in the computer world?) Miracles have happened.

What's a Microprocessor, and What Does It Do?

It's been described more ways than I can count: the "brain" of the computer; the "heart" of the computer; the "camp counselor" of the computer. . . . Why confuse things?

The *microprocessor* is a small black wafer, about the size of a Triscuit. The microprocessor is tightly packed with circuitry that controls a computer's ability to know what to do, and to do it. It's nestled deep inside the computer's system box on a flat green thing called a *motherboard*. Other circuits on the motherboard connect with pins on the microprocessor, and in this way the microprocessor reaches out to more remote parts of the computer (say, the keyboard) and tells them what it has done and what to do now. Over and over again, the microprocessor processes these instructions, all in the inconceivably fast time frame of millions of instructions per second (MIPS).

Jär-gen:

Many different microprocessors hang out inside a computer and assist with menial chores. That's why the main microprocessor, the one that ends in 86, is also known as the CPU (central processing unit)— the replacement for the bulky, desk-sized CPUs back in the dim mists of time. Any old microprocessor, even the CPU, is often shortened to just processor. And, because nerdly types like jargon, they call 'em chips, too—a tribute to the small, thin chips of silicon material used to make the processors.

286, 386, 486: What the Numbers Represent

This chapter will tell you what the first number in most computer ads represent.

Why start here? Well, more than any other single element, these numbers point to how fast and powerful a computer will be and how much it will cost. They're short for bigger numbers (somehow, that doesn't surprise you) that tell you which microprocessor is driving the computer.

Why Do Chip Numbers Always End in 86?

The microprocessors you'll see when shopping for a PC hail from the Intel Corporation's 80*x*86 (eight-oh-ex-eight-six) chip family, a hoary clan whose most prominent ancestor was the 8086 chip used inside the first IBM PC-compatible computers. And, in case this is sounding too consistent to possibly be about computers, the first real IBM-brand personal computer housed not an 8086, but a chip called 8088.

ISTORY

The Altair   Even the 8086 chip claimed an ancestor: the Intel 8080. The 8080 drove the Altair, a personal computer circa 1974 whose name came from a "Star Trek" episode. The Altair had neither monitor nor keyboard —not because they came as extras, but because these extras didn't yet exist. To make it do something, Altair owners spent hours flicking zillions of tiny switches (only to lose all their work when they turned the machine off). Oh, and they had to build it themselves from a kit. Even so, early electronics enthusiasts were well, enthusiastic, about the Altair. Up until then, nobody had thought there was any need for a computer you could use in your house.

Why Are There So Many Chip Numbers?

Each new *xxx*86 number represents a new generation—the higher the number, the more advanced the chip.

That's progress for you. The microprocessor itself is a landmark. Before Ted Hoff thought of putting it on a single chip back in 1969, a computer's central processing unit (CPU) was a boxed unit about the size of a large desk, connected to all the other computer stuff. The old CPUs had to be big, because wired inside were integrated circuits— one to each function—driving the computer. Combining these circuits onto one chip was a stroke of genius. But even then, it took the experts at Intel about four years to realize just what they had.

So What's the Point?

This is all leading up to one thing: You can't stop progress, so don't worry about it. No matter what chip you buy, trust that a bigger, better chip is just around the corner. There's no use waiting for that one chip that everybody will agree is the standard for our time.

Computer chips grow faster, smaller, and more feature-packed with each new generation. And the time between generations grows smaller, too. Chips took a huge leap forward when Intel used a technology called Very-Large-Scale Integration (VLSI) to squeeze a math coprocessor and something called a memory cache onto the 486 chip. The 586, now in development, promises more surprises. And beyond that, Son of VLSI will someday pack up to 1 billion components—a computer's entire central electronic complex—on a single chip.

The PC "river" keeps on rolling, so jump right in. No one ever gained anything from the power of personal computers by waiting to buy one.

Are There Other Types of Microprocessors?

Microprocessor families abound, and each type of chip has a different PC, mainframe, or even supercomputer to boss around. But the 80x86 microprocessor clan is the one that concerns you most right now.

NOTE

What Brand Name Should I Buy? It really doesn't matter what brand chip you buy if you're careful to find out how long the manufacturer's been in the chip-cloning business. A rule of thumb in the computer industry is that the first few products are bound to have some bugs. Wait, don't rush; do your homework and finish reading this book before you buy anything.

HISTORY

Chip Brands.   Until recently, which brand of chip you should buy just wasn't an issue. Intel made the chips for IBM-compatible PCs. And Motorola made the chips for Macintoshes and some other personal computers. That was that. Easy: even for computers.

In the early days, Intel decided to open up its 8086 and 80286 chip technologies by licensing them to other companies. Intel hoped to standardize the industry and create a bigger market, and it did. But Intel stopped its "open" approach in 1985 after it introduced the 80386 chip. Too much money was at stake.

Even after it closed down access to licensing rights, the giant chip maker was challenged by a tiny startup called Advanced Micro Devices (AMD) for the right to use the 386 name on their clone chip. Intel took its case to court, claiming copyright infringement, but the judge ruled in favor of AMD—saying that "386" had become a generic term.

That broke Intel's monopoly on the 386 and caused the company to push its 486 technology even harder. (The ruling also resulted in huge price wars—and big breaks on 386 prices for the rest of us!)

Today, numerous companies manufacture unauthorized 386 and 486 chip clones. Intel has learned its lesson: The 586 won't be the name of its newest chip, according to a quote from Intel president Andy Grove. What will Intel call its new chip generation? It's anyone's guess. Right now it's code-named the P5.

The world can only mourn the passing of the "86" chip lineage: An island of consistency in the normally chaotic computer seas.

In This Chapter, You Learned . . .

Since you're shopping for a PC-compatible microcomputer, you'll be evaluating systems whose chips belong to the 80x86 family.

Because they belong to one family, all these chips are compatible. Even the newest chips can run old software that was designed for older PCs with older chips inside.

Sadly, that doesn't work both ways: Older chips can't handle some of the new software, which may require more *megahertz* (the chip's clock speed), or some of the other design improvements featured in the new chips.

Don't Forget to Ask . . .

- What class of microprocessor is indicated on my software's box?

- If my software requires a stronger class of chip than I can afford, could a less demanding software package do the trick?

Recommendations: _____

_____

- If the chip's a clone (made by a company other than Intel), how long has the chip maker been in business? Does the chip have a good reputation for reliability?

- Is the salesperson knowledgeable, polite, and interested in assessing and fulfilling your needs regarding microprocessors?

Notes: _____

_____

_____

_____

_____

_____

_____

Notes: _____

_____

_____

_____

_____

_____

_____

_____

_____

_____

_____

_____

_____

_____

_____

6

Shopping for a Microprocessor

As you walk through a computer store or thumb through mail-order ads, it's easy to compare features and to decide what monitor or keyboard you want. Microprocessors aren't as easy to peg. They're not very outgoing, because they're too busy doing "important stuff."

The computer's chip is housed deep inside the system box, where it snaps into a socket on the motherboard. (The motherboard is home to some other computer vitals, too. We'll look at those in Chapter 7.)

Even though you can't see it, don't worry; you'll never have to guess what microprocessor's inside a given computer. Computer vendors like to crow about the speed and the power of their systems, if the chip's a powerhouse. Or else they tout the system's affordability, if the chip's a more unassuming type. Either way, you'll see chips like the ones in Table 6.1 proclaimed loudly in ads, signs, and sales pitches.

Here's what it all breaks down to:

Table 6.1   PC Chips on Parade: Bigger numbers mean newer, faster, costlier.

"Street" Name	Chip	Bits	MHz	Comments
(P5) 586	P5 (80586)	32*	66 (+)	*32-bit chip; 64-bit data-path capabilities
486DX2	80486DX2	32	50	The Doubler: doubles 25 MHz clock to 50 MHz
486DX	80486DX	32	25,33,50	Another name for 80486 below; powerful
486	80486	32	25,33,50	Math coprocessor and memory cache on chip
486SX	80486SX	32	20	No math coprocessor; fine for most users
386DX	80386DX	32	25,33,40	Another name for 80386 below; adequate
386	80386	32	25,33,40	A good value; fast enough for most needs

"Street" Name	Chip	Bits	MHz	Comments
386SX	80386SX	32/16	20,25	Less expensive, scaled-down 386
286	80286	16	6–12	Aging technology; rarely seen for sale
088 and 086	8088 / 8086	8 / 16	4.77 / 8	Ancient; first IBM PC and compatible chips

*As of this writing, the P5 was to be a 32-bit chip.

In a Nutshell, What's the Big Difference Between These Chips?

Each chip in Table 6.1 has a *bits* number. Because the function of a computer chip is to process data, it's useful to be able to measure the amount of data a chip can handle at any one time. The word *bit*, which stands for *BInary digiT*, is the basic unit of measurement for describing a chip's data-handling power.

The bit number tells how big a stream of instructions the processor can process. It also tells how many bits of data the chip can move to other key components, like memory and the keyboard.

Think of the early 8-bit computer as a drinking fountain spout, a 16-bit as a bathtub faucet, and a 32-bit as a fire hose. And soon, the 64-bit capabilities of the 586 will clamor for a comparison (a culvert?). Each time a different number shows up in the Bits column, that means that particular type of PC broke the previous bit limit and advanced personal computing just a bit!

Note that the Bits column shows two numbers for the 386SX. Keep reading to see why.

Exactly How Do the 386DX and the 386SX Differ?

The 386SX came about because, at the time, the 386 cost way too much for the average person. When the Intel Corporation designed the 386 chip, one of the improvements they'd made was to beef it up to 32-bit capability.

Soon, everyone wanted a 386 so they, too, could shoot data around in big, 32-bit-wide streams. But only the big-business tycoons could afford one.

Put simply, Intel released a more affordable chip by disabling some of the 386's 32-bit capability. They called the more affordable chip a 386SX.

Jär-gen:

What About the Chips That Have SX, DX, and No Xs at All? In brief, the SX model is slightly less powerful than its brethren labeled DX. And the chips with no X numbers are identical to the full-fledged DX models.

Those of you who'd like to understand just how the two chips differ need to know a little more about how chips work. Bits travel down two data "hoses" on a chip. One's called the *internal data path*, where bits of information get processed. The other's called the *external data path*, where bits of processed information shoot over to the system memory and around the motherboard to other parts of the computer.

Well, to boost sagging 386 sales, Intel decided some people might not need or want a full-size, 32-bit external data path. So, they scaled it back to 16 bits and called it macaroni. (No, they really called it a 386SX.)

It worked. Computer makers bought the hybrid chip in droves and stuck them in cheaper systems that could process 32-bit streams of instructions, just like the 386, yet transfer data around the motherboard in 16-bit streams, just like the 286.

Okay. And the Difference Between the 486DX and 486SX?

Ah, recall the wonders of VLSI technology? Now able to shrink components and connections to new degrees of tiny, engineers managed to cram onto the 486DX chip not only the CPU, but a chip dedicated solely to numerics, called the math coprocessor. (The 486 holds some other extras, too, but right now we're more concerned with the math coprocessor.)

HISTORY

Math coprocessors have been around for years. They cheerfully calculate the national deficit or the fluid dynamics of a boogie board—as long as your software supports the extra boost in power. Until the advent of the 486, if you found your computer balking at big jobs, you went out and bought a math coprocessor. Then you pressed it into your motherboard, if your motherboard even sported the proper socket.

Well, the same people who called the shots on the 386SX decided some 486 users might not have the highfalutin' needs best addressed by a math coprocessor. They took the 486 chip and disabled the math coprocessor. And that's a 486SX.

Current 486SX models run at 20 MHz—a little slower than the true 486 but still fast enough for most computational needs on this planet. The 486SX costs less than the 486, too.

What Else Does the 486 Family Have Over the 386?

Even though it doesn't have a math coprocessor, the 486SX shares with the 486DX some other advantages over the 386. The 486-family chips have a memory-management unit, 8 kilobytes of *cache memory* (an area where the CPU can go to find frequently used data), and a built-in *cache controller*, which speeds the CPU's access to the cache area. This means they remember instructions they've already seen much faster than any other chips.

Also, the 386 runs more slowly, in general, than chips from the 486 family. It takes the 386 three times longer than the 486 and 486SX to do something.

Clock Speeds, Megahertz, 33 MHz: What Does It All Mean?

One more number begs to be compared when you're chip shopping. That's the chip's clock speed, or *megahertz* (MHz) rate. *Hertz* is a measure of cycles, or clock ticks, per second. Megahertz means one million clock ticks per second.

You'll see the chips' megahertz numbers advertised in all sorts of ways at the computer store or in ads: 386SX/25, 386SX–25MHz, and so on. But they all mean the same thing. That modest, unpretentious, even dainty 386SX/25 does its stuff at the rate of 25 million clock ticks per second.

The higher the megahertz number, the faster the chip crunches instructions. Yet a chip's megahertz rate is only one factor of many to consider. As you can see in Table 6.1, one chip can come in several different speeds. But you still need to consider factors like the system bus, memory, hard disk speed and size—there's lots of stuff to think about before you can make the best buy. (Bus and memory will be detailed in Chapter 7 and 8; hard drives, Chapter 10. For more on math coprocessors, see below.)

BOTTOM LINE

The DX2: Doing Double Duty

When is a 486/25 not a 486/25? When there's a 486DX2 chip inside. Intel's *486DX2/50* chip, also known as *The Doubler*, doubles the 486/25's system clock's 25 MHz rate within the CPU. That's a 50 percent reduction in the clock ticks a CPU needs to do something.

How does The Doubler work? Recall the two types of data paths in every microprocessor: *internal* and *external*. A special integrated circuit called the *phase-locked loop* on the Doubler chip allows internal data path speedup of 50 percent. External cache, peripherals, RAM, and other stuff on the motherboard accessed by the external data path are still tied to the PC's standard bus rate (in this case, 25 MHz).

Although the 25/50 MHz Doubler was first, there's a version that accelerates 33 MHz systems to 66 MHz, as well. Intel is planning a 16/32, 20/40, and even a 50/100 MHz Doubler.

Do I Even Need a Math Coprocessor?

Probably not on your first computer. Maybe not even on your second. And you certainly don't need one if you buy a 486, because it already has one!

If you have any doubts, read over some of the user scenarios in Chapter 3. Do any of them sound like you? If you're still not sure whether you need a math coprocessor, turn to Chapter 4 to learn the needs of some of the software you think you'll be running. And if that doesn't tell you, hunt down a computer store or a user group where you can test drive the software you have in mind—with and without the coprocessor.

So, Which Microprocessor Is the Best Buy? It always boils down to what you'll do with the computer. Broadly speaking, buy a 386–33MHz if your programs run under Microsoft Windows. If you plan to do light spreadsheets and mostly word processing with DOS programs, you'll do fine with a 386SX. People with heavy graphics and sound in their applications may opt for a 486SX or even a 486–33.

BOTTOM LINE

What If I Want to Add a Math Coprocessor Later?

If you think you'll need a math coprocessor down the road but you don't want to shell out bucks for a 486 just this minute, be sure to mention your concerns in any information-gathering calls you make to dealers and mail-order houses. Make sure there'll be a place on your motherboard for the coprocessor once you need it.

Will I Ever Want to Upgrade to a Better Chip?

The best way to avoid an unhappy match is to use a little foresight in planning your purchase. That means thinking a bit, now, about how soon you'll want to boost, or *upgrade*, your system's power. (Trust me; you'll want to upgrade. Someday. No matter how fast a computer is you buy today, someday it's going to seem woefully slug-like—fit only for the kids' sticker database.)

Questions to Ask When Buying an Upgradable Model

Ask if its memory architecture will be compatible with the new chip. You'll never have a true 486 if you try to access data from a 386SX memory layout, because the chips differ so in their bit-width capability. You'd hold back the 486 to the 386SX's 16-bit limits. (Check Chapter 7 for more details on bus architectures.) If an upgradable has a 16-bit data path to memory, keep shopping.

Ask if the upgradable comes with flash BIOS. (*BIOS*, covered in detail in Chapter 7, runs the computer's basic operations.) *Flash BIOS* enables you to electronically update these instructions. That makes it easier to tell the rest of the computer there's been an upgrade.

Compare the Cost of an Upgradable Computer

Be sure to compare the cost of upgradable versus non-upgradable models. Buying the basic system and upgrading can cost more than buying the higher-powered system in the first place. Ask pointed questions, such as how long the vendor will sell and support the upgrade card—and your machine, for that matter.

Design Factors Count

Another good question: Just who will perform the upgrade? Will you be performing a brain transplant on your dear old computer? If so, ask how the upgrade installs. If through an expansion card, sometimes you have to remove all the other cards in your system before you can begin. Be sure the design makes sense.

NOTE

A growing trend in system design makes upgrading even easier by leaving the vendor out of the loop later on down the road. The latest upgradables feature motherboards that let you simply pop out the old CPU and snap in the new one. That way, you don't pay for the special CPU upgrade card, but only for the new chip. And you don't have to depend on any particular vendor for the chip.

I know what you're thinking: Why don't they make all computers upgradable with a simple pop/snap of a chip? You can always hope. If you think about it, though, the cost of personal computers would shoot way up if computer makers had to maximize every box's potential for memory, bus, hard drive space and expansion slots, and even extra cooling power—at birth. There's no guarantee everybody would take advantage of these extras, and yet we'd all be charged for them.

Chip Checklist:

Store/ Vendor	System Name	Chip	Bus	Size	Megahertz	System's Brand	Price
___	___	___	___	___	___	___	___
___	___	___	___	___	___	___	___
___	___	___	___	___	___	___	___
___	___	___	___	___	___	___	___
___	___	___	___	___	___	___	___
___	___	___	___	___	___	___	___
___	___	___	___	___	___	___	___
___	___	___	___	___	___	___	___

Don't Forget to Ask . . .

- What class of microprocessor is indicated on my software's box?

- If my software requires a stronger class of chip than I can afford, could a less demanding software package do the trick?

Recommendations: _____

_____

_____

- If the chip's a clone (made by a company other than Intel), how long has the chip maker been in business? Does the chip have a good reputation for reliability?

- Does the system come with a math coprocessor?

- Is there room for a math coprocessor if I decide to upgrade later?

Notes: _____

_____

_____

_____

_____

_____

Meet the Motherboard

I hope you took a good, long breather after Chapter 6. You deserve it. After all, you're only a third through this book, and you already know most of the important stuff about buying a computer.

For instance, you learned that wise shoppers first decide what they want to *do* with their computers; then they find the software that will accomplish their goals. You discovered many different types of software. And you saw which software runs best on the various ranks of PC systems.

In Chapters 5 and 6, you learned that the microprocessor is the first big hardware decision to face. And you're just about to find out what else goes on in the system box.

See? You're almost an expert, or at least you will be once you meet the motherboard. Let's continue by heading back to the store's PC display. We can pry open one of the system boxes and view a motherboard close-up, as well as some other neat stuff.

What's a Motherboard Again?

It's big; it's green; it's the *motherboard*—a nickname for the large printed circuit board underlying everything else in the system box. (See Figure 7.1.) System boxes come in a vertical orientation, too, called a *tower*. Towers have the motherboard along one side. To see what that looks like, turn the book on its side and look at Figure 7.1. There.

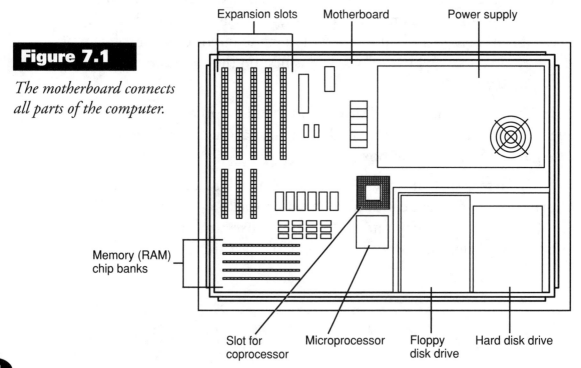

Figure 7.1

The motherboard connects all parts of the computer.

Expansion slots   Motherboard   Power supply

Memory (RAM) chip banks

Slot for coprocessor   Microprocessor   Floppy disk drive   Hard disk drive

The most important thing to know about the motherboard is that everything else in your computer plugs into it—including the micro-processor.

You've heard the comparison: The microprocessor is the computer's brain. If so, the motherboard's the skull. Choose carefully. Scull trans-plants are possible, but best saved for experts.

The motherboard houses other essential components, like ROM and the BIOS, expansion slots, and DIP switches.

What's ROM?

Even the self-important microprocessor has a boss: the ROM chip. *ROM* stands for *read-only memory,* a permanent set of instructions etched onto the ROM chip. These instructions set the computer's basic personality.

Computer manufacturers can store many types of instructions in ROM. But once in place, a ROM chip can't be altered. That's why it's called read-only: The instructions can be read but not written over with other instructions.

Where Does BIOS Fit in?

BIOS stands for *basic input-output system.* It is one of the groups of instructions preprogrammed onto a ROM chip. The BIOS' job is to see the computer through the identity crisis it suffers each day.

When you flick your computer's power switch first thing each day, the machine panics. It can't do a thing without instructions. Right away, the BIOS kicks in and reassures the computer.

You: Flick.

Computer: "Argghh! That electric jolt again! Now they expect me to *do* something."

BIOS: "Get a grip. You're computer X, with BIOS X, and you have memory X, hard disk X, floppy drives X and X. Your operating system is MS-DOS X.X."

Computer: "Uh, right."

BIOS: "Now go load your operating system."

Computer: "Right. Thanks, BIOS. I needed that."

The whole process of turning on a computer is known as *booting up.* That's when the machine performs something called *bootstrapping,* a term that comes from the old expression "to pull yourself up by your own bootstraps." (You never knew computers were so folksy!)

Expansion Slots and Expansion Cards

Expansion slots on the motherboard provide a way to connect various devices, like monitors or scanners, to your computer. Figure 7.2 shows an expansion card plugging into a slot. Each device plugs into a card, which then plugs into an expansion slot. A special cable connects the device to its card inside the computer.

NOTE

A device usually comes with a card, but some make you select a card separately. For instance, few monitors come with a video card. Whatever method, don't forget that you need the proper connectors and cables for each device.

Shopping guidelines for ROM and BIOS? Not too many, since you don't get to choose the ROM chips that come in a particular PC. Even so, ask what BIOS version the PC is running. Get the latest version possible, since different BIOSs can affect the performance of otherwise similar PCs.

For example, certain new hard drives won't work with a BIOS that was made before 1989. In the unlikely event that your new computer sported such a BIOS, you wouldn't be able to upgrade to one of these hard-drive models.

A few hardy souls perform their own BIOS upgrades. But this pertains to those readers who are thinking about buying a used computer. (Shiver.)

BOTTOM LINE

Figure 7.2

Expansion cards for new devices connect, via expansion slots, to the motherboard.

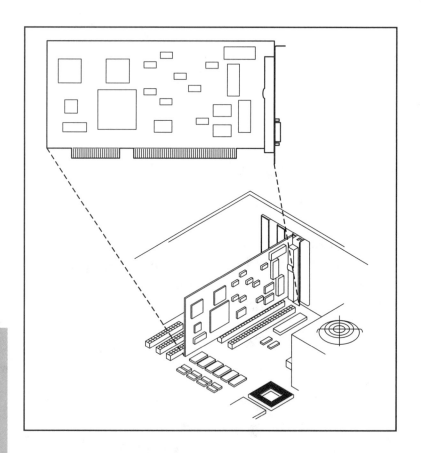

Jär-gen:

You may see the terms interface card, card, daughterboard, add-on board, or even just board used in place of expansion card. It's all the same thing—a neat new toy for your computer.

How Many Expansion Slots Do I Need?

Just as you can choose what CPU or how much RAM will go in your computer system, it's up to you to decide how many expansion slots your new system will hold. Since a computer's expansion capacity is rarely mentioned in ads or placards, it's something you'll have to ask about. Generally, the more expansion slots you get, the more you'll pay (and the bigger your system box will be).

NOTE

Adding new devices via expansion slots is one way you can protect yourself from computer obsolescence. You can easily expand your basic computer system as your needs grow or as new technology develops. And, as wise computer owners will tell you, extra slots don't stay empty for long.

What's the Difference Between 8-Bit Slots, 16-Bit Slots, and 32-Bit Slots?

You know that microprocessors differ in how big a stream of data they can handle in a given time. Well, expansion cards differ, too. As with microprocessors, higher bit widths mean a bigger data stream flowing to and from the card. Faster access. More time for the fun stuff.

When shopping, don't ask how many expansion slots come with the system, but rather how many will be left after adding a video card, a mouse, and other basics.

BOTTOM LINE

What Size Expansion Slot Is Best?

Expansion devices come in a range of bit-sizes, as shown in Figure 7.3. Make sure your motherboard holds at least one 32-bit and several 16-bit slots.

NOTE

Bigger slots can hold smaller cards; the opposite's not true.

Do Expansion Slots Have Something to Do with the Expansion Bus?

An expansion card's speed is often measured in bus size instead of bit-width. *Bus* is short for *data bus*, the circuitry on the motherboard where data travels to and from the microprocessor. If you think of an expansion card as an extension of the motherboard, the card's data bus counts, too. The entire grouping of expansion slots and circuits is called the computer's *expansion bus*.

8-bit slots   16-bit slots   32-bit slot

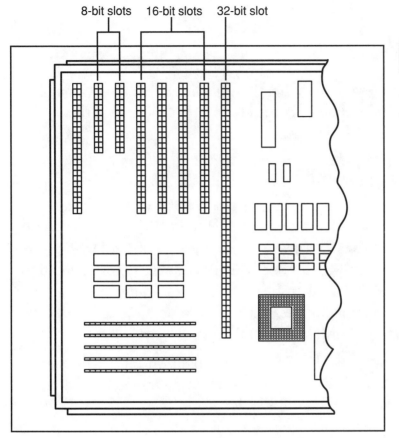

Figure 7.3

Expansion slots range in size from 8-bit to 32-bit widths.

 ISTORY

EISA, ISA, et cetera . . .   When 32-bit microprocessors came on the scene, computer manufacturers found that the rest of the system lagged behind the blazing chips. What good was a fast microprocessor when data couldn't travel from memory or devices through the data bus any faster than before?

The manufacturers set out to resolve this dilemma, but differences of opinion arose as to how best to revise the PC's bus architecture. The original AT bus is called *ISA*, for *Industry Standard Architecture*. IBM's new plan was dubbed *MCA*, for *Micro Channel Architecture*. But MCA involved costly licensing fees, so nine other computer makers joined forces and agreed to develop and support their own new world order: *EISA*, or the *Enhanced ISA* bus.

The EISA bus is compatible with older expansion cards, which is a real advantage. (MCA, now supported by some third-party manufacturers, isn't compatible.) On the downside, it used to cost a lot more than ISA. Prices may be leveling out as you're reading this. If so, or if you want to remain compatible with as many expansion cards as possible, EISA's the way to go.

Some Ads Say Local Bus. What's That?

Local bus is a new technology that links the microprocessor directly with expansion cards so they can run at full speed without bogging down in the data bus. So far, only video cards come with the local bus option, and it hikes up the cards' prices another $150 to $300 dollars. Hard drive cache controller cards are next in line for local bus technology. Since it's new, there aren't any real standards; instead a host of vendors are tinkering with their own, proprietary local bus models. A tip: wait for this one.

What Are DIP Switches?

DIP switches are tiny switches found on the motherboard and also on expansion cards. Hardware devices, like printers or modems, can sport these, too. When you add newcomers to your system, it's customary to flip the switches until everyone feels at home.

NOTE

You manipulate DIP switches to adjust various settings on your computer, but it's wise to leave them alone unless you can faithfully recreate their original settings when you're done playing.

In This Chapter, You Learned . . .

The motherboard, housed in the system box, connects all the computer's components. ROM chips contain the BIOS, which directs your computer's start-up routine.

Expansion slots are part of the motherboard's expansion bus. These slots provide a place for you to add new devices to your computer via expansion cards. Of all the different expansion bus standards, EISA's the one to watch.

Dip switches are found on expansion cards, devices, and the motherboard. You can change their settings to coordinate new devices with your system.

Motherboard Checklist:

Store/ Vendor	System Name	BIOS	Brand/ Version	Expansion Slots/Sizes	Bus
————	————	————	————	————	————
————	————	————	————	————	————
————	————	————	————	————	————
————	————	————	————	————	————
————	————	————	————	————	————

Don't Forget to Ask . . .

- What's the latest possible BIOS version I can get?
- Have problems been associated with particular BIOS brand/version?
- Is the expansion bus EISA, ISA, or MCA?
- How many expansion slots will remain free after the system is configured to my tastes?
- Are any free slots blocked by brackets or other hardware?
- Are the expansion slots 8-bit, 16-bit, or 32-bit?

Notes: _____

_____

_____

_____

_____

_____

_____

_____

Don't Forget RAM, Another Type of Memory

The motherboard holds another key to a computer's speed and power: *random-access memory*, or *RAM*. The amount of RAM on a computer, along with the power of its microprocessor and the size or speed of its hard disk, determines how well your software will run.

What Is RAM?

RAM gives the microprocessor a place to dump all the data, the instructions, the input mumbo-jumbo, and the stray socks it's not using at the moment. Safe in RAM, the information waits patiently until the busy microprocessor comes to retrieve it. This RAM holding tank eases the chip's load, so processing takes place more quickly.

Recall from Chapter 7 that after ROM's BIOS prodded it into action, the microprocessor loaded its operating system. Loaded it where? Well, the microprocessor itself doesn't have that much memory space. And ROM chips are off-limits—no new stuff can be written there. So the operating system was "written to" RAM, for the short term. RAM, unlike ROM, can be read from and written to.

RAM is notable for one other thing. It's fast, because all the data access or storage takes place electronically. Electronic streams of bits and bytes (pronounced *bites*) move much more rapidly than bulky, slow mechanical devices.

Random Access means the microprocessor takes an equal amount of time to access any one of RAM's memory cells. These cells are organized in a special, two-dimensional grid. It's like a wall of post office boxes, or a bingo card. The microprocessor gets the scoop on a piece of information's address (B-12), and goes to the B column and down to the 12 to grab it from that cell. Bingo!

RAM Is Volatile; ROM Is Not

When is information not safe in RAM? When the computer is turned off. Because it's electronic and not mechanical, RAM needs constant refreshing by a stream of electrical pulses. Those pulses come through your ordinary wall socket, up the power cord, and into the system box. When that stream shuts off—for instance, when the computer's turned off or accidentally unplugged—RAM empties its contents. Swoosh! That's why they call RAM *volatile memory.*

That explains the existence of two customs: turning off a computer during an electrical storm, and saving your work to floppy disks and hard drives (see Chapters 10 and 11).

How Is RAM Measured?

Like software, hard disks, and the mileage left on your teeth, RAM is measured in bytes. One *byte* equals eight bits, and a *bit*, as you'll recall from Chapter 5, is the smallest unit used to measure data.

A byte holds a character of memory, equivalent to one letter of the alphabet. Each of RAM's cells holds a single byte and gives this byte a particular memory address, ready for the microprocessor's retrieval, as Figure 8.1 shows.

The byte is a pretty small unit of measurement. Bytes are so small that even in the early dawn of computers people tended to clump bytes into thousands, or kilobytes (K, KB or Kbyte, for short). A *kilobyte* equals 1,024 bytes.

Early PCs held 64K of RAM. Many computers sold today have at least 640K RAM. Most PCs count their RAM capacity in *megabytes* (meg or MB), however. One MB of RAM equals about a million

Don't even consider buying a computer with less than 1MB of RAM onboard. At least two megs is vastly preferable, and four or more is a good idea if you want to run graphical programs like Microsoft Windows.

BOTTOM LINE

bytes, or 1,024K. The fastest PCs on the market, the 386 and 486, can access 4 billion bytes (gigabytes, or GB) of memory.

Each of RAM's cells holds a single byte of information at a specific memory address, in a system similar to a grid of post office boxes.

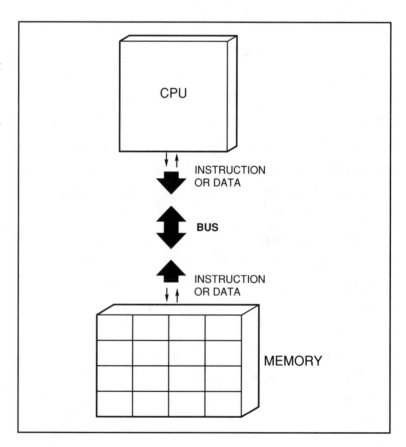

Memory Cells Can Be Addressed Several Ways

You may see the terms interleaved memory, static-column memory, page-mode memory, and row/column memory. These design differences are attempts to increase the speed at which the CPU accesses, or addresses, the memory cells.

Interleaved memory divides it into equal portions and processes them alternately. Static-column memory finds one column to store data, then stores subsequent data in that same column. With page-mode memory, memory accesses occur back-to-back in blocks called pages. And row/column memory is a bingo-card-like, grid-accessing method.

What's the Dealer Mean by Static and Dynamic RAM?

RAM chips come in two styles. *Static RAM chips* are faster and more expensive than the other type, *dynamic RAM chips.*

RAM Capacity Few computers come fully loaded with RAM. But the computer you buy should have sufficient RAM chip slots, so you can add more later. Once the motherboard's RAM banks are filled, even more RAM can be added via RAM expansion cards.

A 386 motherboard should accept a minimum of 16MB of additional RAM. A 486 should allow for at least 32MB of main memory, plus a 256K RAM cache.

Ask about a computer's memory configuration. RAM chips come in different sizes; the motherboard should accept both 1MB and 4MB memory chips. Avoid the cheaper, 16-1MB chip layouts.

BOTTOM LINE

Jär-gen:

The memory chips you'll encounter most are the dynamic RAM chips, which are often referred to as DRAM chips (pronounced d-ram).

Three RAMs: Conventional, Expanded, and Extended Memory

Early computer designers lacked foresight: They never thought a PC would be able to use more than 640K of RAM. Even today, that early barrier's known as *conventional memory.*

Later on, computer designers came up with special memory expansion boards that could fool the computer into thinking it was grabbing the new memory from the old, conventional memory range. This is known as *expanded memory.*

Extended memory chips plug directly into chip slots on the motherboards of newer computers, as Figure 8.2 shows. Oddly, when it accesses extended memory, the computer still fools itself into thinking it's using older, expanded memory—except in the very latest, most advanced software.

NOTE

Make sure the computer you buy sports extended memory. More and more of today's advanced software is beginning to take advantage of it.

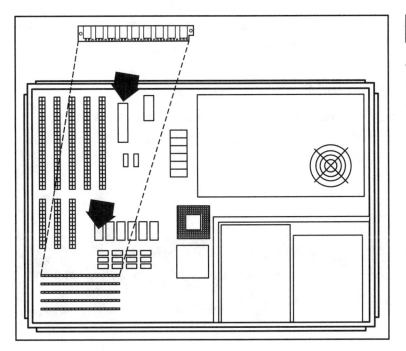

Figure 8.2

A bank of RAM chips on the motherboard of a 386 PC.

What's a RAM Cache?

A good feature to look for is a *RAM Cache*, also called *cache memory*. It's a bundle of fast memory chips on the motherboard that serves as a bridge between the fast microprocessor and the slower main RAM. By predicting what instructions are likely to be needed next, RAM caches reduce the computer's *wait state*, the time it spends waiting for something to do in between instructions.

If you see a computer advertised as *zero wait-state*, chances are, it has a RAM cache. A 64K cache is sufficient for mid-sized systems.

Are They Serious? Shadow RAM?

It sounds sinister, but *shadow RAM* is just a feature to speed microprocessor access to the BIOS by loading BIOS directly into *fast RAM* when the computer's turned on.

Shadow RAM may cause memory conflicts with other software. Make sure you know whether your computer has it, and if so, how to disable it.

In This Chapter, You Learned . . .

RAM chips provide memory for the computer to store stuff in while working. So the more you get, the better off your computer will be.

The minute you turn off your computer, this volatile RAM empties itself, which explains why people store their work on floppy or hard disks.

RAM Checklist:

Store/ Vendor	System Name	RAM On-board	RAM Capacity	Config- uration	RAM Cache	Shadow RAM
_____	_____	_____	_____	_____	_____	_____
_____	_____	_____	_____	_____	_____	_____
_____	_____	_____	_____	_____	_____	_____
_____	_____	_____	_____	_____	_____	_____
_____	_____	_____	_____	_____	_____	_____

Don't Forget to Ask . . .

- How much RAM comes on-board the system?

- What RAM configuration does the motherboard feature? Can it use both 1MB and 4MB chips?

- How many additional megabytes of RAM can I add?

- What does the dealer charge for RAM? (Mail-order may be preferable.)

- Does the system have a RAM cache? How big is it?

Notes: _____

_____

_____

_____

_____

_____

_____

_____

_____

_____

_____

_____

_____

_____

_____

_____

_____

_____

_____

_____

Notes: _____

_____

_____

_____

_____

_____

_____

_____

_____

_____

_____

_____

_____

_____

_____

_____

What Else Does the System Box Hold?

As you saw in Chapter 7, the thick computer case shelters some impressive parts. You'll be grateful you understand what they do, once you go shopping. But before you can buy the best system, let's see how the rest of the case's contents work together.

Besides, one look around the store reveals lots of different-looking cases. Why are there so many configurations? A computer's a computer, right?

What Are Ports?

Even the sketchiest computer ad lists ports as part of the system package. *Ports* are connectors on the back of the system box where you plug in a printer, modem, or other devices. They're called ports because they're gateways into your computer's innards, as Figure 9.1. shows.

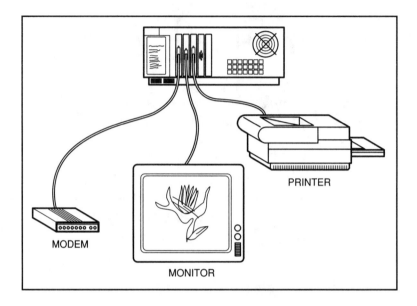

Figure 9.1

Ports are gateways into your computer's innards.

MODEM

MONITOR

PRINTER

How do ports differ from expansion cards inserted into expansion slots, as in Chapter 7? They're actually not that different: It's just that some of the expansion slots on a computer come prefitted with one or more serial interface cards to make a serial port, and a parallel interface card for a parallel port.

Rather than separate cards, it's common for the vendor to insert a multifunction card inside a computer. A *multifunction card* holds a combination of ports, usually two serial ports and a parallel port.

Some PCs sport a separate game card, or you can buy one yourself and plug it into a spare expansion slot. Then you have a game port, and you can plug in a joystick and blast invaders until it's time for "Star Trek" reruns.

The important thing to remember about ports is that each type of port handles devices made only for it. So you can't plug a joystick into a serial port, for example. When buying printers, modems, or tape-backup units, be extra careful to match device with port type.

Serial Ports

Serial ports provide a place to connect serial printers, a mouse, or a modem, to name just a few serial devices.

A serial device gets its name because of the way it transmits instructions—one bit at a time, over one wire, or serially. Figure 9.2. shows typical serial connectors which typically come in 25-pin, and sometimes 9-pin, connectors.

Parallel Ports

Parallel ports transmit information over eight wires (in 8-bit, or 1-byte, chunks). They're faster than serial ports in the same way you saw that 32-bit data buses transmitted information faster than 8-bit buses.

A parallel port usually attaches to a parallel printer, although other parallel devices exist. Parallel ports and devices connect with 9-pin or 25-pin plugs, as in Figure 9.3.

Figure 9.2

Serial and parallel ports sport 9-pin or 25-pin connectors.

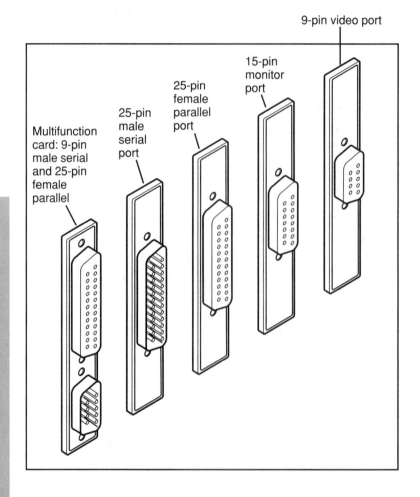

9-pin video port

15-pin monitor port

25-pin female parallel port

25-pin male serial port

Multifunction card: 9-pin male serial and 25-pin female parallel

Jär-gen:

Serial Ports *Serial ports should be clearly labeled at the back of the computer. The label usually says serial or sometimes COM (for communications port), since many people connect serial (external) modems to this port. Another name for serial port is RS-232 port (computer people enjoy talking in numbers and do so at the slightest provocation). Parallel ports are sometimes called LPT, short for line printer port.*

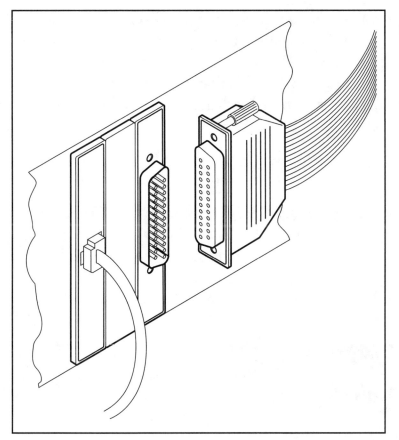

Figure 9.3

Cables plug into connectors on the back of the computer.

SCSI (Scuzzy) Ports

SCSI stands for *small computer system interface*. Since they're even faster than parallel ports, they're used to attach high-capacity hard drives, CD-ROMs, and tape-backup units.

And yes, they're really pronounced *scuzzy*. Most PCs don't come with one installed (Macintosh-brand personal computers do). The neat thing about SCSI ports is you can chain up to eight SCSI devices off one port. The downside to SCSI ports is that all SCSI devices aren't compatible with the port or with each other, so you have to be careful when selecting SCSI add-ons.

Drive Bays

Drive bays are large slots with racks inside the system box. Drive bays hover over the motherboard and harbor hard drives and floppy drives. They come in either vertical (stacked drives) or horizontal (side-by-side) orientation.

> *When shopping, look for drive bays that can be accessed from outside the computer.*

Plan for future needs by asking how many spare drive bays the system offers. Later you may want to add hard or floppy drives or even an internally mounted CD-ROM unit. Some tower cases sport up to seven extra drive bays!

Power Supply

No sense in owning a super hot-rod computer if its *power supply* can't keep up. Power supplies are measured in watts and range in strength from 80 to 300 watts. Even though every computer system comes fitted with a power supply, make sure it's powerful enough, especially if you plan to add things later on, such as tape-back-up units.

When shopping, ask if the power supply will be sufficient if you choose to expand the machine to its maximum capacity. Table 9.1 provides some power-supply guidelines. As in every area of life, use common sense: If a Desktop Model you're looking at offers gobs of drive bays and expansion slots, go with the recommendation for a Tower Model.

Table 9.1   Adequate power supply for expanded systems.

Slimline Unit	*Desktop Model*	*Mini-Tower Unit*	*Tower Model*
80–100 Watts	100–150 Watts	100–150 Watts	200–300 Watts

Buy a Power Strip

A computer's not just something you plug into the nearest extension cord. Before deciding where to put it, ask yourself if there's a free outlet nearby.

Plug your new computer into a power strip, or maybe spring for a surge suppressor. Both appear in Figure 9.4.

A *power strip* is like a heavy-duty extension cord. One end plugs into the wall, and the strip sits on the floor, ready to supply your components with juice. Power strips provide seven or eight sockets—one for the system box, printer, monitor, modem, lava lamp, boom box. . . . You won't have any trouble filling up the spare sockets.

Surge Protection

Power strips may offer surge protection. If so, they will shield the computer's sensitive parts against fluctuations in electrical current, which are known as *power surges* or *power spikes*. Not all power strips guarantee protection, so it's wise to make sure you know if you have it or not. (Some people don't opt for surge protection, opting instead to save their work to disk frequently and turn their computers off in electrical storms.)

Because even the slightest power cuts can mean hours of lost work, many experts recommend plugging a computer only into a special surge suppressor unit, shown in Figure 9.4. Some offer separate power switches for each component. You pay for surge protection: Units average $25 to $130.

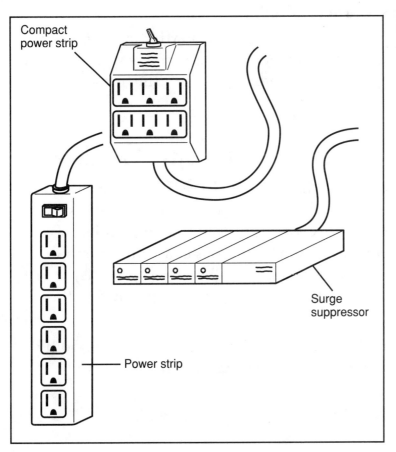

Compact power strip

Power strip

Surge suppressor

Figure 9.4

Plug your new computer into a power strip or a surge suppressor unit.

Finally, make sure the computer comes with a heavy-duty, three-pronged power cord.

The Biggest Systems Need to Keep Their Cool

Large, powerful computers such as the 486–50MHz model generate lots of heat. Ask about cooling methods. Some models sport a second cooling fan in the power supply; others use a heat sink method. Some high-powered computers offer both.

FCC Approval: Critical, but Easy to Overlook

As computers become more powerful, they leak strong electronic signals that interfere with other transmissions over the airwaves. To minimize electronic interference, the Federal Communications Commission (FCC) regulates electronic emissions that escape from PC cases. Systems rated Class B emit the least interference, so they're approved for home use. Class A systems pass muster only for office or industrial use.

One exception to this rule: Super high-powered PCs (486–50MHz models and above) aren't required to meet Class B approval (go figure!).

Portable computers come rated Class B only. And yes, the Federal Aviation Administration is on record as saying they do believe laptops pose "a potential for interference to aircraft avionics."

Make sure the computer you buy is clearly marked Class B Approved.

What Case Style Is Me?

Check out the variety of PC systems crowding the computer store's floor, as in Figure 9.5. There's the desktop model, the sexy portables and notebooks, slimlines, and the hulking tower case. There's even an all-black Darth Vader Special—very sleek. But what's the best case to buy?

Computer cases have come a long way from their bland, desktop-hogging, boxy forebears. Small-footprint computers save space and look tidy, but they forfeit expansion slots, drive bays and other room to grow. The same is true of slimline models, which offer side-by-side disk drives. Tower models offer lots of room for expansion but take up floor space.

Figure 9.5

Computers come in a variety of styles and colors.

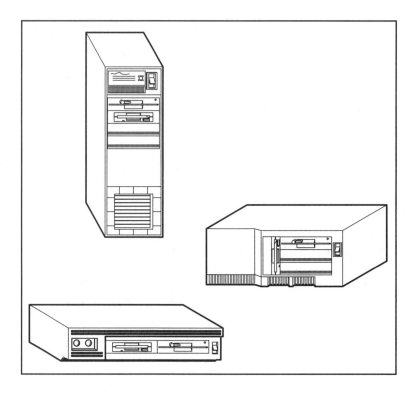

A Shopping Note! Look critically at the various models available. Assess the amount of room you now have and how likely you are to expand your system later. Then try to strike a compromise.

Looks are important, it's true. And that all-black model would look great in your high-tech computer nook. But the question to ask yourself is: "What components will combine to build the best solution to my current and near-future computing needs?" As you continue reading this book, keep that question on your lips. The system-box dilemma is sure to solve itself.

The Touch Test

When you think you really like a system, it's time to give it the touch test. Sit down. Make yourself as comfortable as can be expected, considering the salesperson's glaring over your shoulder and the system next to you is occupied by a 5-year-old who's busy programming the Space Shuttle's next orbital.

Mail-order readers can forget about such distractions—but can't touch-test the system. Instead, compare system photos in advertisements to Figure 9.6 to make sure a system's buttons and switches are in the comfort zone.

Floppy Drive Location

Floppy drives are almost always found within easy reach along the front of a computer system. You'll be reaching for the floppy drives often; double-check to be sure they're in the best spot for you.

Figure 9.6

Buttons and disk drives should be within easy reach on a system box.

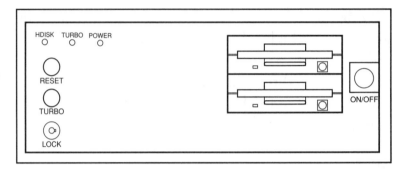

The Power Switch

Check the position of the power switch. A front switch is easiest to reach and allows more range in where you put the system (against a wall, for example). Side switches mean you won't turn the computer off accidentally—but they're not as easy to reach. A power switch along the back of the computer will keep you limber, but ultimately it's a pain.

The Reset Button

The reset button gives you a way of emptying RAM and resetting the system. Why would you want to do that? Well, some programs ask you to reset the computer in order to complete the installation process. You'd also want to press the reset button when the computer is acting up and won't do anything you tell it to (this pesky occurrence is called *freezing up*, or *crashing*).

A reset button keeps you from having to turn the computer off and on again. The alternative's called a *cold boot* and is to be avoided at all costs (cold booting throws a giant strain on the computer's electronic components). Obviously, you'll want this button to be within easy reach. Front placement is best, but recessed, to avoid accidental reset-ting.

The Turbo Button

A turbo feature lowers or raises the megahertz rate with the touch of a button. Often, an indicator light on the system box tells you when you're in turbo mode. Why wouldn't you want to run at maximum speed at all times? Well, a few programs, notably older computer games, won't work at the highest speeds. The turbo switch toggles from fast to slow(er). Chances are you won't be using this feature often, so it's okay along the side.

LED Read-Outs

Some models sport *Light-Emitting Diode (LED)* read-outs that moni-tor megahertz rate. Other lights advise hard drive and turbo status. Think of where you'll place your new computer once you get it home, and make sure these lights are easy to see.

In This Chapter, You Learned . . .

Expansion cards that come already installed in a computer's system box provide at least one parallel port and often two serial ports to connect the most basic devices, such as printers and external modems, to your computer. You can add more specialized ports, such as SCSI or game ports, if you purchase specialized devices. The number of ports that come with a computer are clearly listed in ads or at the store. Ports are exclusive creatures; you have to be careful when shopping to match port with device type.

Computers vary in the number of drive bays they offer, as well as in the strength of their power supplies. Check to make sure these meet your needs. And don't forget to buy a power strip, or even a surge suppressor unit.

All systems need FCC approval; you're better off with a Class B-approved computer to minimize radio interference. The more powerful systems need adequate cooling, too. And it's essential that your case fit your available space, as well as your expansion needs. Finally, no purchase is complete without the touch test.

Chapter 7 Checklist:
What Else Is in the Box?

Ports Checklist

Store/ Vendor	System Name	Parallel Ports	Serial Ports	Game Port	SCSI Port
_____	_____	_____	_____	_____	_____
_____	_____	_____	_____	_____	_____
_____	_____	_____	_____	_____	_____
_____	_____	_____	_____	_____	_____
_____	_____	_____	_____	_____	_____

Don't Forget to Ask . . .

- Power supply wattage?
- Cooling measures?
- FCC rating visible?
- Drive bays accessible from outside the computer?
- Drive bay rails included for expansion?

- Mounting brackets included?
- Power cord included?
- Comfy button arrangement on the box?
- On/off switch easily reached?
- Configuration: Tower, Desktop, Small Footprint?

Notes: _____

_____

_____

_____

_____

_____

_____

_____

_____

_____

_____

_____

Notes: _____

_____

_____

_____

_____

_____

_____

_____

_____

_____

_____

_____

_____

_____

_____

_____

_____

Floppy Disk Drives and Diskettes

The last few chapters provided a look at almost all the parts inside a computer's case. Yet, no matter how many cool gizmos it has, without any software, the computer sits there blankly. In this chapter, you'll learn about the mechanism by which the PC accesses a software's instructions. That's the PC's *floppy-disk drive*, also found inside a computer's case.

You already know that software programs are instructions that tell your PC what to do, and they come in files on media called *diskettes* (or just *disks*), packaged in software boxes you purchase. But how does the software get to where the hardware can use it?

When you install a new program, you take its disks from the software package and insert them into the PC's floppy disk drive one at a time, removing the old one before inserting the next disk, as in Figure 10.1. As you insert each new disk, you then tell MS-DOS to copy the data from the disk to your PC's hard drive (more about hard drives in the next chapter). As you remove the disks (also called *removable media*), you put them back in the software box for safekeeping.

Figure 10.1

The PC accesses new software through disks in its floppy disk drives.

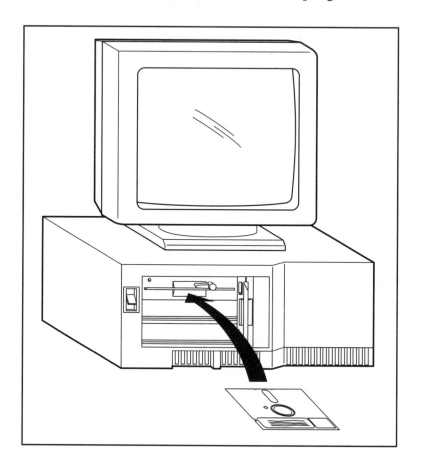

Now the program's there in your PC, ready for the microprocessor to use.

Chapter 3 compared a software disk to an audio cassette tape. Without music on tapes, the stereo remains silent; without software on disks, the PC can't do anything.

A PC Reads from and Writes to Disks

Floppy disk drives are mechanical devices that are able to "read" floppy disks, just as a stereo's tape player can "read" the music recorded onto audio tapes. There's another important similarity between disks and audio cassettes. While many audio tapes come prerecorded with an artist's music, you can also buy blank tapes where you can record stuff you want to play back later. Same with disks. You buy software "prerecorded" onto disks, but you also buy blank disks to store your work on, for "playing back" later.

Remember discovering back in Chapter 8 how RAM provides a place for the microprocessor to store data and instructions it isn't using at the moment? Well, recall what happens to RAM when you accidentally unplug your computer: All the *volatile* memory goes swoosh into data heaven. Floppy disks (and hard disks) are where you save your work while you're using your PC. Before quitting for the evening, you also *back up* all your work onto floppy disks you keep just for that purpose.

ISTORY

But I've Seen Disks Before and They're Not All That Floppy! The hard cases on the newer, 3 1/2-inch disks make a complex subject even more puzzling: Why do they call them floppy disks?

If you take an older, 5 1/4-inch disk in hand and bend it a bit, it gives: hence, it's *floppy*. At least it's floppier than the *hard* disks, which store data in a similar way, yet are housed in a fixed, seldom-removed drive inside a computer case.

The word floppy *really* came from comparing hard disks with the super-ancient 8-inch disks that prevailed back in the Cretaceous Era of Disks. Those suckers could really bend. Some computer gurus say it's floppy because the media inside the soft 5 1/4-inch and hard 3 1/2-inch disks is pliable plastic, similar to the audio tape your car stereo dribbles at you when it's mad. (You'll see lots of weird theories in the world of computers, most of which you can safely ignore.)

Two Sizes, Four Capacities

Floppy disks and disk drives come in two sizes, either 5 1/4-inch or 3 1/2-inch versions, as Figure 10.2 shows. Some people call the 3 1/2-inch versions *micro floppy disks*. (You don't have to say this silly word if you don't want to.) On your new PC, you choose what size floppy drive you want and what capacity disks it handles.

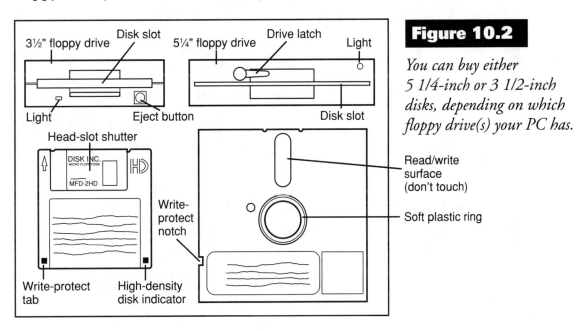

Figure 10.2

You can buy either 5 1/4-inch or 3 1/2-inch disks, depending on which floppy drive(s) your PC has.

Like RAM, a disk's capacity is measured in bytes. Disks come in four different byte capacities, measured either in kilobytes (K) or in megabytes (M or MB), as shown in Table 10.1.

Table 10.1   Disk capacities in kilobytes and pages of text.

Density	5 1/4-inch	3 1/2-inch
Double Density	360K (120 pp.)	720K (240 pp.)
High Density	1.2MB (400 pp.)	1.4MB* (480 pp.)

*IBM offers a 3 1/2-inch diskette drive that formats to 2.88MB.

Even the lowest-capacity disk can transfer hundreds of pages of text, program instructions, pictures, and even sounds to and from a PC, as Table 10.1 and Figure 10.3 show.

How Can I Tell the High-Density and Low-Density Disks Apart?

Unfortunately, there's no reliable way to tell the high- and low-density 5 1/4-inch disks apart, except perhaps by looking at the label on the box or the diskette. Some low-density disks sport a reinforcing hub ring around the center hole.

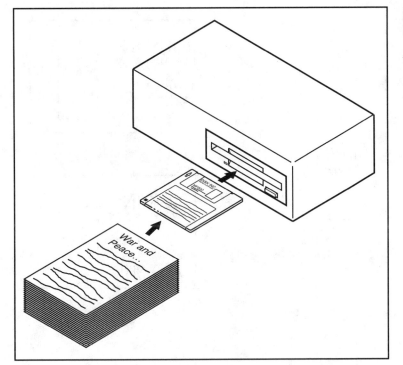

Figure 10.3

A floppy disk can hold hundreds of pages of text and data.

The 3 1/2-inch disks look different, as in Figure 10.4. Often the high-density ones have an HD symbol to the right of the *head-slot shutter* (the part you stick into the computer's drive). The head-slot shutter may say MFD-2HD under the brand name. If all else fails, turn the disk so the head-slot shutter's facing you and right side up. A high-density disk has an extra square hole in its bottom right corner.

Figure 10.4

Here's how to tell if a 3 1/2-inch disk is high-density.

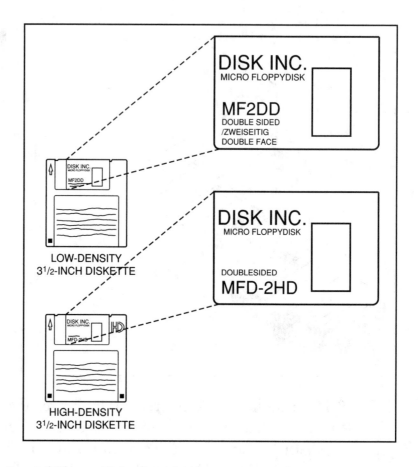

What If I Need a Second Floppy Drive Later?

If you buy a PC with only one floppy drive and later decide you need another, don't despair. You can always have a second drive added, or add one yourself, with the help of a book on upgrading your computer. Just make sure you buy a PC with enough available *drive bays* (spare drive compartments in the system box) for later additions.

Where to Stock Up on Disks

Mail-order companies are the least expensive sources for disks. Some mail-order houses sell nothing else. If you take this route, know that the mass-quantity, El Cheapo brand in the big plastic bag really does differ in quality from the more expensive brand-name disks. Your data's safe enough, but each disk may not hold the full capacity of data marked on the label.

Also, as computers have been with us for a longer period of time, people are starting to discover that the stuff they stored on their very oldest disks is slowly fading away. It's no one's fault—it just happens. Always keep plenty of blank disks on hand so you can make backup copies of your most cherished backup disks every year or so.

Which Floppy Drive Should My New Computer Have? You'll get the best buy if you purchase a PC with two floppy drives: one high-density 3 1/2-inch and one high-density 5 1/4-inch drive. Here's why: High-density drives can read both low- and high-density disks. The reverse doesn't work: Low-density drives can read only low-density disks.

Most software comes on one size of disk; rarely does a package contain both. Although most software publishers offer to exchange disks for the right size, this is done through the slow U.S. mail, and often you have to pay about $10 extra for the privilege.

BOTTOM LINE

Where to Store Your Backup Disks

When you buy your computer, buy a disk storage unit like the one in Figure 10.5. Make copies of your MS-DOS (or whatever operating system you bought) disks and store them in here. Also, copy important files like CONFIG.SYS, AUTOEXEC.BAT, and your setup information to a special disk, and store it in your new disk holder. Ask a friend to find the files and back them up for you if it's confusing.

Do I Need One of Those Head-Cleaner Disks?

You may have seen ads or even computer magazine articles on cleaning your floppy drive's read/write heads with a special cleaner kit. This is not necessary and can really mess things up in there. If something does go wrong with your drives and your dealer finds out you're cleaning them, your warranty may be void. There's no such thing as preventive maintenance with your floppy drives!

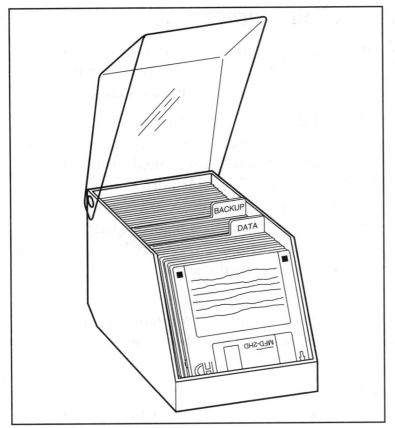

Figure 10.5

Buy a disk holder to protect your backed-up data.

In This Chapter, You Learned . . .

Software holds the instructions that prod a PC into doing something useful. Since software generally comes on floppy disks, the most common way a PC accesses new programs is through its floppy disk drives.

Floppy disks and disk drives come in two stylish models: 5 1/4-inch and 3 1/2-inch versions. Each version can be further divided into two different capacities: higher capacity (room for more data and program stuff) and lower. Whether you buy a 5 1/4-inch drive or a 3 1/2-inch model, if you buy the lower capacity drive for your PC, you are stuck using low-capacity, or low-density, disks. The higher capacity drives, although more expensive, offer much more versatility because they can work with both low- and high-capacity disks.

Try to buy a PC with spare room for at least one additional floppy disk drive, because adding an extra drive is a common way people upgrade, or remodel, their PC systems once they've owned them a while.

Because floppy disks hold not only purchased software but also your work, or data, you should buy plenty of extra disks and use them regularly to back up anything you and your PC have accomplished together.

Chapter 10 Checklist:

- Have I checked my preferred software's requirements for disk drives?

- Have I considered buying one high-density 3 1/2-inch and one high-density 5 1/4-inch drive?

- Have I bought enough disks to get me started? A disk storage unit to protect my backup disks?

- Does the PC have room for additional floppy disk drives?

Notes: _____

_____

_____

_____

_____

_____

_____

_____

_____

Hard Disks Aren't So Hard

In case you haven't noticed, a certain theme has popped up in every chapter so far (it's okay to sing along): To buy the best computer, you first need to decide what tasks you want to perform, and then you need to find the software that can help you accomplish these tasks. Then buy the hardware that runs that software best. Tra-la.

Nowhere is this more true than when you choose a hard disk drive for your PC.

A Faster, Easier Way to Store More Stuff

You read in Chapter 10 that floppy disks provide a more permanent way than RAM to store data and programs. But a larger, faster, more convenient storage place exists for your programs and all the work you do with your computer: a hard disk drive.

Compared to a hard disk, floppies don't hold that much data. Floppy drives are among the most mechanical components, too, so they're agonizingly slow.

Because your PC's hard disk will hold the software and data you use regularly, choose one only after you have a good idea what software you'll run. Your choice of software will affect two important shopping decisions:

- How much the hard disk holds

- How fast the hard disk operates

Also, since "bigger" and "faster" almost always translate into "more expensive," know that the hard disk you choose will make a big difference in the price you pay for your PC.

How Does a Hard Disk Work?

Like floppies, a hard disk's capacity is measured in megabytes (MB or M). A hard disk drive works like a floppy drive, except the disk and drive are one unit. There's another difference: You can't tell if there's a hard drive in a PC just by looking at the front of the system box, as you can with floppy drives (check out Figure 11.1.). You'll see only a hard disk indicator light, which comes on whenever the hard disk's being accessed.

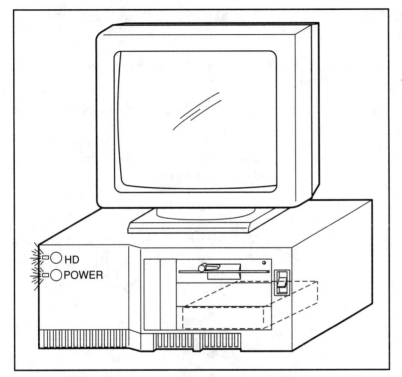

Figure 11.1

A glance at the system box's front won't reveal the presence of a hard drive.

The hard drive unit fits inside the system box, in the same kind of drive bay as the floppy drive(s). The disk's made of the same magnetic recording material as a floppy, but is *fixed,* or permanently sealed, in its drive. A disk stores your data on one or more platters, stacked up like pancakes. The bigger the hard disk's capacity, the more pancakes, in general, although some of the newest models squeeze all their capacity onto a single platter.

Each platter's accessed by a *read/write head* that is connected to a *head arm*—sort of like a bizarre jukebox. The platters spin while the head hovers over them, as Figure 11.2 shows. The head floats on a cushion of air that's 20 times thinner than a human hair.

Figure 11.2

A hard disk spins inside a fixed case, where read/write heads access it.

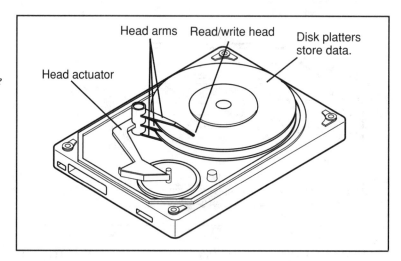

Head arms   Read/write head   Disk platters store data.

Head actuator

When a hard disk (or a floppy, for that matter) comes off the assembly line, it's smooth and clear, a blank slate. In order to help the read/write heads find your data, a disk needs to be divided into sections, or *formatted.*

Formatting a disk lays down on its smooth surface the physical addresses for data, known as tracks and sectors. In the case of hard disks, each platter surface is subdivided.

Tracks can be likened to the concentric grooves on a 33-rpm record album (does anybody remember these?). Well, imagine taking the album and etching thin pie slice lines into it. These pie shapes further divide the tracks into sectors, which further organize the disk in preparation for data storage. Even though sectors around the outside of the pie cover more physical area than the ones around the inner pie, each sector stores the exact same amount of data, usually about 512 bytes.

Each track, and each sector on that track, is numbered. When you tell your PC to store a data file on the disk, the PC gives your file its own address on the disk, expressed in clusters. A very small file will take up at least one cluster, usually four to eight sectors, while a large file may sit in many clusters. Either way, the read/write head knows just where to find your data, thanks to tracks and sectors!

When you tell your computer to retrieve a file, the DOS software gives special signals to the hard disk

A typical PC system usually comes with its hard drive preformatted. Check with the dealer to ensure yours will be ready to roll (so to speak).

When you buy floppies, you format them yourself (although you can pay more and buy preformatted floppies—not a best buy, since formatting is so easy!). Both hard drives and floppies are formatted by way of a command in your operating system, usually MS-DOS, that's invoked by typing (not surprisingly) **FORMAT**. *(Get a tech friend to show you how to use FORMAT, but never format a disk without knowing you'll erase any data that's there.)*

BOTTOM LINE

controller, telling it exactly where to access the cluster. You can actually hear your hard drive spinning away, grabbing the data you need and transferring it into RAM. Impressive, eh?

Other Types of Storage

In addition to conventional hard disks, you may see tape backup units and CD-ROM drives offered for sale. Here's a quick look at each of these.

Tape Back-Up Units

A tape backup unit automates the laborious task of backing up data and programs from today's huge hard drives. The unit is easily installed in a spare drive bay, or external units can be positioned near the system box.

Tape backup units are great for small businesses and home systems with critical data to protect, because no one has to sit in front of the computer for hours plugging in floppies for backup. However, they're expensive: low-end models range from $350 to $1,000, while faster, more reliable models range from $1,500 to $2,500. The units are also rather noisy, and the backup can take a long time to complete.

Not all tape backup units are compatible with one another; if you're depending on another tape backup unit at another site, shop carefully to ensure compatibility.

Removable Hard Drives

Removable hard drives are cartridges that plug into a slot, much like floppy disks fit into a disk drive. They combine the storage capacities of a hard drive with the portability of a floppy disk. If you have compatible drive units in two different computers, for example, you can transport your entire hard disk from one computer to the other.

Removable hard drives are expensive: $500 to $2,000, depending on capacity, speed, extra disks, and so on. They're also bulky and heavy: even the lightest drives tip the scale at 3 pounds. External models (which most are) can take up a parallel port. And finally, these hard drives are slower and less efficient than regular hard drives.

CD-ROM Drives

CD-ROM drives play compact disks, just as your stereo's CD player does. However, instead of music, computer programs are recorded on CD-ROM disks. CD-ROM stands for Compact Disk Read Only Memory; the "read only" part refers to the fact that, like music CDs, you cannot write data to them—you can only read it.

CD-ROM discs save interminable disk-swapping when installing large software programs. Many popular programs are being distributed on CD-ROM discs, such as CorelDRAW!. Lots of other interesting CD-ROM discs are available, including multimedia software, entire encyclopedias, and shareware libraries. With the proper software, CD-ROM drives can also play audio discs through your PC's speakers or through headphones.

CD-ROM's failings are speed (although a RAM buffer feature may lessen the agony) and price. It is difficult to find a CD-ROM drive for under $300, and most decent ones are in the $500 range. When shopping for a CD-ROM drive, make sure the drive you select is compatible with multimedia programs (ask the salesperson). If you get one that's too slow for multimedia, you'll be stuck using it for simple data retrieval and music listening.

How Much Disk Storage Space Do I Need? The minimum hard drive for a moderate user is an 80MB model. If you plan to use graphics, sound files, or Windows and Windows-compatible software, spring for 100 megs, although 200MB would cover your future needs better. A power user would jump right into the 350MB–600MB range.

BOTTOM LINE

How Much Does the Hard Disk Hold?

Even the smallest hard disk holds about 20 times more megabytes of programs and data than the highest-capacity floppy disk. If you're shopping for a pre-configured PC, it's important to verify not only how big its hard drive is, but details about the drive's controller, access time, transfer rate, physical size, MTBF, and brand name.

How Fast Is It?

Even the older hard drives spin at 3600 rpm, ten times faster than a floppy drive. Two measurements must be considered when you're comparing hard drives: a drive's *average access time* and its *data transfer rate*.

Average Access Time

The *average access time* is the time it takes the drive head to reach and read a random cluster on the disk. Access time is measured in milliseconds (ms), one-thousandth of a second. The lower the number, the faster the access time.

A fast hard drive is anything less than 20 ms. Here are some general guidelines: a 286 PC should be able to access hard drive data at between 20 and 30 ms; a 386 PC between 16 and 20 ms; and a 486 PC between 15 and 18 ms.

Data Transfer Rates

Data transfer rate refers to how quickly data moves from the hard drive to your PC's RAM memory. A slow data transfer rate can bog down even the fastest access time. Hard drive transfer rates vary with PCs, but the higher the number the faster the rate. A 386/33, or higher, will sport a high transfer rate—700K per second is fast. For 286 systems, anything over 500K/sec. is fine.

MTBF

One last number begs to be compared, and that's the drive's *Mean Time Between Failures,* or *MTBF,* given in the number of hours a drive should work without any problems. An MTBF of 25,000 would be 25,000 hours of working without *crashing,* the term given to hard disk failures. Look for 20,000 hours or above. Use caution here, for this rating comes from the manufacturer.

Do I Need a Hard Drive in My System?

Originally, floppy disks were the only means of storage available to computer users. Because a floppy drive's read/write head physically contacts the disk, they rotate slowly, hitting about 360 rpms (revolutions per minute). Computer designers figured there had to be a better way, so they sealed up the disk along with the reading/writing mechanism and stuck it inside the computer's case. Voilà, the first hard drive.

Early hard drives were unreliable and expensive. That's why, until fairly recently, many people didn't bother buying a hard drive for their PCs. Hard drives cost too much, these people reasoned. Only big businesses needed them, they told themselves.

Of course, four friends of mine do not own hard drives. These folks (writers all) seem only slightly irritated by their lack of mass storage. Just the same, they all sing the same lament: "no hard drive." Once they do buy a hard drive, my friends will curse themselves for waiting so long.

You'll find yourself hamstrung pretty quickly without a hard drive. The time waiting for floppies to spin goes by torturously slow. And picture yourself swapping floppies every time you want to spell-check a report or save updates to your database. What's more, programs are quickly outgrowing even the largest hard drives. A ten-second voice sequence in one of today's advanced computer games takes an entire 360K disk. Finally, the price of a good hard drive starts at around $3 per megabyte. A hard drive is no longer a luxury.

So, no—the computer store's alarm won't blare if you try to leave without a hard drive in your new PC. But my conscience won't rest unless I do my best to persuade you how much you need one.

What Do Half-Height and Full-Height Mean?

Hard drives commonly come in these sizes. Half-height, about 1 1/2 inches high, is the standard. Full-height, an older standard, is still used for the largest capacity drives. Some computers sport third-height bays. Tiny 1.3-inch drives are just appearing in the marketplace.

If you're planning to add a bigger hard drive to your PC later, and perhaps add devices like internal CD ROM drives or tape backup drives (discussed later in the chapter), make sure you have the right-sized bays available for the models that have caught your eye. To be safe, look for models with at least one full-height bay open.

What Brand's the Best?

Hard disk manufacturers come in and out of vogue. Check with user groups, computer sales staff, and computer magazines for any current hard-drive "horror stories."

Different Types of Hard Drives

Hard drives use a *controller* to direct data access. The controller technology determines the drive's type.

The most popular type of hard drive is the IDE drive, which stands for *Intelligent Drive Electronics*. Older, ST-506 drives (named for their original way of accessing data) had separate controllers. The IDE's controller has been integrated onto the drive itself. Another type of drive, *ESDI*, or *Enhanced Small Device Interface*, is the current high-end favorite; it offers high data transfer rates and large capacities.

The SCSI drive is becoming increasingly popular. You might recall the SCSI interface from Chapter 9's discussion of ports. As with other SCSI devices, up to seven SCSI drives can be "chained" together. (There'd be a whole lotta storage goin' on!) The SCSI adapter card you add to your expansion slot typically contains a cache memory device.

Table 11.1 provides a quick hard-drive type reference chart.

Table 11.1   Types of hard drives.

Type	*Features*
ST-506	Older, slow
	Cheaper

continues

Table 11.1   Continued

Type	*Features*
ESDI	Large capacity Fast Expensive
IDE	Controller on drive Good Value
SCSI	Device chaining Controller and processor on adaptor card Expensive Good in multiple-drive systems

Here's a Techie Tip   Look for drives that use a voice-coil actuator to position the read/write heads. These mechanisms are found on the better drives. Steer clear of earlier, stepper motor head positioners, as they lose alignment over time, they can grate more against a drive's head and affect a drive's overall performance.

BOTTOM LINE

Hard Disk Cache Memory

As you learned earlier in the chapter, the speed of a hard disk depends partially on its data transfer rate. But what if you could avoid some of the data transfer entirely?

A *cache controller*, pronounced "cash" controller, cuts down on the amount of data transfer that needs to be done by stashing data in its high-speed memory chips. Then, if you need that same data again, it's available without going back to the hard disk.

Cache controller cards come in two bus styles: ISA and EISA. ISA cards typically can be upgraded to 16M of RAM, and the EISA cards hold roughly 24M of RAM. As you know from Chapter 7, the ISA bus design is more common on PCs, while computers that sport the enhanced ISA, or EISA, are more expensive, as are EISA-compatible cache cards. Unless you have abnormally heavy hard disk use in mind, you'll find an ISA-compatible cache sufficient for your needs.

Some SCSI adapters offer cache capabilities. It's becoming more common to see some type of buffers onboard IDE drives, as well. Read-ahead buffers help, but better still are read/write or segmented buffers.

Built-in Caches

Some newer hard drives come with built-in cache capabilities, speeding up data access considerably. Be sure to ask about a hard disk's caching abilities before you buy. These come in two flavors: read-ahead buffers or read/write buffers, also called segmented buffers. This last type is the best type to have.

A less expensive way to benefit from a disk cache is to install special software that uses some of your PC's RAM as a disk cache. Ask a techie friend about this neat use for RAM.

What Is a Stacked Hard Drive?

You might hear the term *stacked hard drive* at user group meetings or when talking with friends who have PCs. Stacker is one of a number of commercial products that squeeze down the size of data on a hard drive so the drive can hold more—sometimes up to twice its former capacity. Hard drives that have been compressed in this manner are referred to as "stacked."

Although Stacker and products like it work well for people who have underestimated their storage needs, it's more a "fix" or last resort before springing the "big bucks" for a new, larger hard drive. Be sure to carefully estimate your storage needs (then double this number).

CD-ROMs, Removable Hard Drives, and Other Types of Storage

Space doesn't permit extended discussions of all the other ways to store data. Here's a brief summary of some other options.

Tape back-up units automate the growing task of backing up work from today's huge hard drives. These are easily installed in a drive bay or can be left as external devices. They're essential for desktop publishers and others involved in data-intensive applications.

As magneto-optical and removable hard disks become more popular, their prices will fall. That has already happened with CD-ROM drives, which work like a musical compact-disc player to read prerecorded software on high-capacity CD-ROM discs.

Because software publishers increasingly distribute their programs on CD-ROM discs, they merit some space here. With CD-ROM drives, access time (also measured in milliseconds, or *ms*) determines both performance and price. Very slow drives measure around 1,000 ms. Newer, faster drives come close to 300 ms. (That compares to 20 ms on a typical hard drive.)

As with hard drives, a RAM buffer can help speed access time. Check out the drive's audio capabilities (most can play music CDs) and make sure it comes with audio software—not just a demo. When shopping for a CD-ROM drive, read articles and talk to other users for their feedback.

After-Sales Support

A hard drive is one of the most expensive PC components you'll buy. Ensure a long-lasting, happy relationship with the manufacturer or dealer by checking on the type of support you'll receive.

Dealer and Manufacturer Support

The dealer should support all warranties and technical questions. A manufacturer may not offer toll-free support or may limit support to a Bulletin Board System, or BBS (see Chapter 2 for more on BBS support). However, mail-order vendors specializing in hard drives usually have their own, highly knowledgeable technical sales and support staff. Look for toll-free telephone support.

Documentation

Manuals and set-up specs provide important information you may need later, if not at first. If you buy from a dealer, your drive should be installed and ready to go, but the manuals are good to have around. Mail-order vendors provide their own documentation as part of a drive package. Get all the written information you can.

BBS Support

If your hard drive manufacturer does offer BBS support, count on speedy access to documentation updates, free downloadable disk utilities, and technical support. Talk with other customers about their experiences.

In This Chapter, You Learned . . .

Knowing how hard disks work will help you choose the best one. After reading this chapter, study performance reviews in recent computer magazines, and choose the model you want in your system.

As in all PC decisions, let your software plans guide you in choosing a hard disk.

Chapter 11 Checklist: Hard Disk Data

Now that you've learned about hard disk specs, jot down any decisions you've made about the hard disk you want. If you read any magazine

articles that discuss specific brands and model numbers, you can write
them down here, too.

Hard Drive: _____

Capacity: _____

Brand: _____

Model#: _____

Speed: _____

Access/Transfer: _____

Controller Interface: _____

Price (or estimate): _____

Notes: _____

_____

_____

_____

_____

_____

_____

Part IV: Outside the PC

Now you finally get to see why this book harped so much on expansion slots. The world is full of goodies to buy and stick inside your new PC. Credit cards ready? Charge . . . !

First, we get to head back to that luscious monitor aisle (only this time, we get to peek because we know what we're doing). Then there's video cards, that crucial, other half of the picture (so to speak).

Keyboards count as being outside the PC, too, as you'll see when the fun ones come out of hiding. Then there's mice, trackballs, and many other toys (just try to look serious when you tell your family you bought a mouse). Modems and monitors round out the tour (and deplete your charge card's limit for the next millennium).

The Monitor Aisle

Pay no attention to those swirling, colorful screens! Seductive and enticing, a state-of-the-art video display sells PCs like nothing else. It's the trump card used by PC stores and mail-order ads to tempt people like Bob and Bernice Bungle into impulse buys.

Ahem! All eyes this way. . . . Shall we continue?

So far, we've covered the components inside the PC. This chapter focuses on the most noticeable part outside a PC: its video display, or *monitor*. The monitor provides a way for you and the computer to communicate. You see your work and the computer's responses to your commands on the monitor.

*Most books on shopping for a computer tell you more about choosing between video standards than about selecting a good monitor. This book gives step-by-step instructions on buying both a video card **and a** monitor.*

To learn more about letters like VGA, EGA, SVGA and the like, flip over to Chapter 13, "Video Modes and Adapter Cards." To learn how to buy the best monitor for your money, stick around.

HISTORY

Monitor Time Line, or Alphabet Soup　While reading, glance at the monitor time line in Figure 12.1. The earliest *monochrome*, or single-color monitors, *MDA*, displayed text in one color, but no graphics. A color monitor released at the same time, *CGA*, could display 16 colors total, either four at a time in low resolution or one color with a crisper image. A *Hercules graphics card* enabled fairly crisp monochrome graphics. *EGA*, the next standard, allowed 16 colors with an even crisper image. *VGA, Enhanced VGA*, and *Super VGA* (today's standards) offer at least 256 colors and photographic-quality images. Details on each of these standards, plus tips on which to buy, appear in Chapter 13.

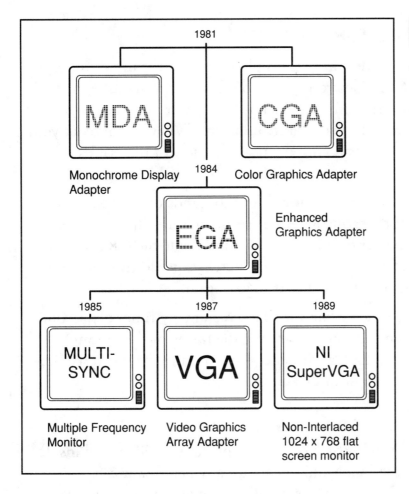

Figure 12.1

Monitors have advanced through the ages.

How Does a Monitor Work?

Just as on a TV set, everything takes place inside a vacuum—the *cathode ray tube*, or *CRT*. Electron guns shoot beams through the tube to scan the inside of the monitor, which is lined with tiny phosphors that glow as they're struck by these electron beams. When you look at your screen, you're actually watching the peaceful glow of thousands of phosphors.

A color monitor features hundreds of thousands of groups, or *triads*, of three phosphor dots: one red, one green, and one blue dot. Color monitors also come with three electron guns inside the CRT: one for each color in the triad. When a beams increases its electron rate, the triad takes on the hue hit by the strongest beam.

Each beam hits the screen many times per second, continuously scanning the inside of the monitor. If you look at the side of the monitor, you can see the subtle scan flicker.

Jär-gen:

Like other PC devices, a monitor connects to an expansion card inside the computer, see Figure 12.2. A monitor's expansion card is called a video adapter card, video card, or sometimes, a graphics card.

A Monitor and Its Video Card

A monitor is only as "good" as the video card inside the PC. Monitors are usually *downward compatible*. That means it's usually possible to run a new color monitor with an older, less-advanced video card. But the results will be crude.

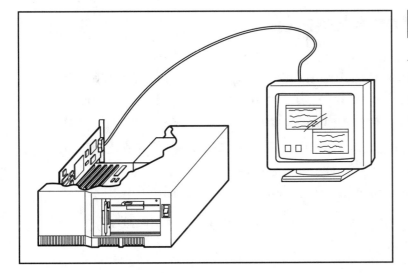

Figure 12.2

A video card inside a PC controls the monitor's display.

Think of the monitors we meet in this chapter as if their corresponding video cards were "driving" them. In Chapter 13, you'll see why most people buy a video card that corresponds to the monitor they buy.

What Monitor Is Best for Me?

There are lots of factors to consider before picking out a monitor—there's no universal answer. The rest of this chapter will introduce you to the important concepts—and help you decide what you need.

Color or Monochrome?

Computer monitors come in two basic styles: *color* and *monochrome.*
You can choose a monochrome monitor with either amber/black or
green/black hues. These inexpensive models are still on the market.
They display sharp text and are adequate for very simple applications.

Color monitors come bundled with most preconfigured PC systems
today. They display a spectrum of colors, commonly 16 or 256 at
once, depending on the monitor/video card combination.

The shopping tips discussed in this chapter pertain mostly to color
monitors.

Do I Need Color?

You don't need a color monitor to get your work done, unless your
application involves color desktop publishing, computer art, or graphic
design. On the other hand, a color monitor enlivens the many hours
you'll spend deep in computing sessions. Color is fun. Most business
software uses color to highlight functions or otherwise ease computing
tasks. In fact, Microsoft Windows and Microsoft Windows software
are much harder to use without color . . . and these programs demand
a monitor that's capable of graphics.

Paper-White Displays

Paper-White monitors provide extra-crisp, black-on-white displays used in specialty fields like desktop publishing and computer-assisted design (CAD). The display technology behind these often-oversized beauties represents an advance over color monitors, so expect them to be much more costly than a more mundane, monochrome model.

Text or Graphics?

Monitors display in two modes: *text-only* or *graphics*. (In Chapter 4, you saw some software in these modes.) Color monitors can display both. Today, very few monitors are text-only. Even monochrome monitors can display single-color graphics with a Hercules graphics card installed in the PC.

Of course, text-only monitors, if you can find one, are dirt cheap because they're not very versatile. If at all possible, however, spend the extra money and get a graphics monitor. Later, you'll be glad you did.

What Resolution?

Resolution determines how crisp an image looks on a given monitor. Four factors decide a monitor's resolution: *pixels, dot pitch, convergence,* and *refresh rate*.

Perhaps a fifth element is the most important of all: your subjective judgment. If you don't think a monitor looks that good, all the numbers and benchmarks in the world aren't going to change your mind.

What Are Pixels?

One of the biggest factors affecting resolution is the number of *pixels* that run across and down the screen. Pixel is short for PICture ELement. The more pixels, the sharper the picture.

Although a monitor is advertised as having a given "resolution," that's a maximum, theoretical number based on the best possible video card connected to that monitor. The actual number of pixels in a given display is determined by the software and the video card—not by the monitor alone.

For example, video cards of the VGA standard enable VGA or Super VGA monitors to display 640 x 480 pixels. A Super VGA video card enables a Super VGA monitor to display images with a crisp 800 by 600 resolution or even higher, but a regular VGA monitor would still be limited to 640 x 480, even with this souped-up Super VGA card attached.

NOTE

Check Chapter 13 for more on video cards and the resolutions they provide.

What Is Dot Pitch?

The color monitor's red, blue, or green electron beams hit their corresponding dot color with the help of a Swiss-cheese-like shield called a *shadow mask*. Tiny holes in the mask guide the beams, so the "blue" beam hits the blue dot, for example.

The distance between the mask's holes is known as *dot pitch*, measured in millimeters (mm). Dot pitch determines how grainy or tight the picture will be. Look for a dot pitch of .28 mm or less. Smaller screens in particular look much more focused with a tighter dot pitch.

What Is Convergence?

When all three electron beams hit a triad evenly, a monitor is said to have perfect *convergence*. Differences in the alignment of the electron guns or a distortion in the shadow mask can throw this off, causing color imperfections and a blurry looking screen.

Ask the dealer to show you the monitor displaying a pure white background. If the monitor looks pinkish or bluish, ask to see another model by the same manufacturer. If it's still off, look at another brand.

What Is Refresh Rate?

A *refresh rate* is the rate that electrons scan from screen top to bottom to restore the tiny phosphors. Refresh rate, also known as *vertical scanning frequency,* is measured in hertz (Hz). The higher the hertz, the less flicker you'll see on the screen.

Look for refresh rates above 70 Hz. The big-screen monitors require even higher refresh rates; anything below 90 Hz will cause noticeable flicker and eye fatigue.

Multi-Scan or Multi-Frequency Refresh Rate

All graphics monitors have two frequencies: a *vertical scan rate* (see above) and a *horizontal scan rate*, the rate at which a line draws across the screen. Each graphics mode requires different frequencies. *Multi-scan* monitors, also known as *multisync*, or *multi-frequency*, can adapt to suit any scanning frequency and are compatible with a wider variety of graphics standards.

If a monitor's billed as multi-scan, make sure it's able to switch back and forth between a variety of

If you're planning to run only newer software, or don't plan to switch modes, you may not need the features of a multi-scan model.

BOTTOM LINE

modes—not just one or two. Look for automatic re-sizing when the resolution switches from one video mode to another. Some monitors only offer manual switching. Look for a monitor that has a broad range of horizontal and vertical scanning frequencies: from 30 kilo-hertz (kHz) to 64 kHz horizontal and 50 hertz (Hz) to 90 Hz vertical.

How Software Affects Resolution

Before you sink $1,200 into the finest monitor in the store, remember this: it's the software that creates those dazzling images. If the software you plan to use does not support your monitor's fancy Super VGA modes, you're no better off than the guy down the street with a regular VGA monitor.

However, support for high-resolution video modes like Super VGA is becoming more and more common in software packages. Even if most current software can't take advantage of it, shoppers with an eye to the future should investigate Super VGA, discussed in Chapter 13.

Interlaced or Non-Interlaced?

Interlaced means the monitor's electron beams scan alternating lines on the monitor, a method of displaying images which speeds up the re-fresh rate of cheaper monitors. Non-interlaced monitors scan the entire screen at once, and they're becoming the standard.

Look for a non-interlaced monitor, which won't flicker and hurt your eyes as much as interlaced models.

BOTTOM LINE

Big Screen or Standard Size?

If your application requires you to see two pages of a document at once, as in desktop publishing, or to see many programs simultaneously in Windows, consider buying a large-screen monitor. These monitors measure 20 inches or more, but you'll pay for the added convenience: They run between $2,000 and $4,000. Make sure you have enough desk space for one of these honkers, too.

NOTE

A compromise between the standard 14-inch monitor and the huge expensive ones is a 15- or 16-inch model. These usually cost less than $1,000.

Other Monitor Issues

Besides the major factors you've learned about so far, there are a number of "extras" to look for in a monitor. While not as performance-critical as resolution or color, they do make a difference, especially after you get the monitor home and start using it.

Flat Versus Curved Screens

Flat-screened monitors are quickly becoming standard (see Figure 12.3). These screens reduce glare, a major source of eye fatigue. Expect to pay more for the flat screen than the rounded one.

Anti-Glare Coating

Increasingly, models offer anti-glare coating to combat sore, red eyes. Inspect these models closely to make sure the coating doesn't degrade the color quality or image sharpness.

> *To be prepared for the future, buy at least an 800 x 600 resolution, .28-dot pitch, non-interlaced Super VGA color monitor with a refresh rate of 70 Hz. This monitor, along with a complementary SVGA adapter card, can keep up with anything your software can dish out—right now and for the next few years.*
>
> **BOTTOM LINE**

NOTE

If your monitor gives you glare problems, you can buy a special anti-glare screen that fits over the glass of your monitor. These $25 glass plates reduce glare and eyestrain significantly, but are not as attractive, durable, or effective as built-in coating.

Figure 12.3

Flat screens reduce glare that can cause eyestrain.

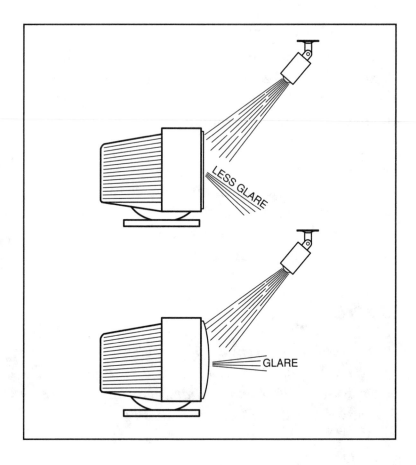

Low Radiation

If you're concerned about monitors emitting radiation, look for compliance with the Swedish MPR-2 standard. Radiation studies are inconclusive at this point, so protection's not guaranteed, but you might feel better knowing that you're doing all you can to lessen your exposure to electromagnetic rays.

Easy-To-Use Controls

Ideally, the monitor's controls should be along the front, where you can reach them easily. Some newer models offer digital controls, with buttons instead of knobs for more precise tuning of contrast, brightness and sizing. The most advanced monitors offer adjustable tint and LCD status readouts, as Figure 12.4 shows. These fancy features may not be worth the extra price you'll pay.

Tilt/Swivel Base

Make sure you can turn the monitor and tilt it to your optimum viewing angle. Add-on products that accomplish the same thing are available; they're recommended by computer-health experts as one way to prevent a sore neck while computing.

Figure 12.4

Some monitors sport front controls and LCD readouts advising your graphics mode.

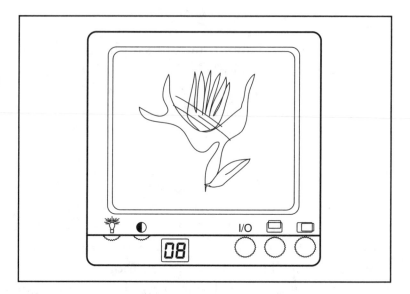

In This Chapter, You Learned . . .

Monitors come in either monochrome or color models. Color models correspond to several video card standards, discussed in Chapter 13. Check a monitor's resolution, size, and control layout before you buy.

In deciding between color and monochrome, keep your present and future software requirements in mind. Search current PC magazines for reviews and comparison articles, and be sure to talk with other users to see what they use, and why. Finally, visit a computer store and try out color versus monochrome for yourself.

Today's advanced games and other entertainment software won't run without a color display. And, paired with a color printer, a color monitor enables you to take full advantage of high-end business software—including future-trends like presentation graphics and multimedia applications that combine animation, sound, and even video.

Chances are good that you'll choose a color monitor, but it will be an informed decision—not the result of a wide-eyed stroll down the monitor aisle!

Chapter 12 Checklist:

When comparing various monitors, keep these criteria in mind:

Monitor Type _____

Model# _____

Price _____

Screen Size _____

Maximum Resolution _____

Dot Pitch _____

Scanning Frequencies _____

Refresh Rate _____

Non-Interlaced? _____ Yes _____ No

Don't Forget to Ask . . .

- Does the monitor flicker obviously when I glance at a point along its side?

- Does a multisync model automatically re-size at different resolutions?

- Does any glare-proofing impede visibility?

- Does the monitor come with all cables and connectors?

- Does the salesperson recommend any special brand of video card to go with the model(s) I like?

Notes: _____

_____

_____

_____

_____

_____

_____

_____

Notes: _____

_____

_____

_____

_____

_____

_____

_____

_____

_____

_____

_____

_____

_____

_____

_____

A Bevy of Video Cards to Max-Out Your Monitor

In Chapter 12, you learned that a monitor was the most visual way for a user to communicate with a PC, and for the PC to communicate back. Since no monitor can function without a corresponding video adapter card inside the PC's expansion slot, consider this a "companion" chapter to Chapter 12.

This chapter details the various PC graphics cards. You will learn to decipher the mumbo-jumbo you'll encounter when making the important decision of what video card and monitor to buy for your PC.

Resolution Revolution

Like the monitors they control, video cards have improved through the years. Early color graphics modes look primitive compared to today's. Although speed and colors count, the *resolution*, or image sharpness, enabled by current video cards really points to the advances in PC displays.

Chapter 12 explained how a monitor's advertised resolution is a theoretical number, something like 640 by 480 (the numbers vary depending on the type of card). This number stands for the maximum number of *pixels*, or picture elements, the monitor can display across and down. The higher the numbers, the sharper the picture.

Resolution's a Group Effort

Although maximum resolution is important, a monitor's true resolution depends on two other factors, as Figure 13.1 shows. First, the monitor's video card must be able to reach that same maximum resolution. Second, a software program must be able to recognize and make use of this resolution.

Resolution Evolution

Higher resolutions display clearer, more realistic images on your monitor. As monitors and cards have progressed in quality, they've driven advances in software, input devices, and even printers. This section will tell you about the major kinds of video cards, from the oldest technology to the newest.

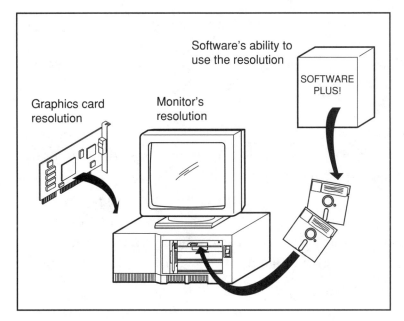

Figure 13.1

The resolution you can achieve on your monitor depends on the capabilities of the monitor, the video card, and the software.

MDA, Plain Vanilla

The earliest standard, *MDA*, offered a clear, monochrome text display at a resolution of 720 by 350 pixels. This was a great improvement over the TV sets and terminal displays available to the earliest PC users.

Hercules Graphics

In 1982, an enterprising grad student developed a monochrome graphics card so he could use his monochrome PC to write papers in his native Thai alphabet. When a major software package started to support it, the card gave rise to a new standard, *HGC* or *Hercules Graphics Card.* Hercules cards enabled graphics at a 720 by 348 resolution. This monochrome graphics standard is still on the market.

CGA, or "C" for Crude

As it grew more affordable, it's amazing how many users flocked to a crude, blurred, blocky-looking standard called *CGA,* or *Color Graphics Adapter.* CGA offered a few different graphics modes, depending on how many colors were displayed. The most common resolution was 320 by 200 pixels (quite a step down from monochrome) in four dreary colors: cyan blue, weird magenta, yellow, and black. Reading text while in this mode made deciphering the Rosetta stone seem easy.

Enter EGA

The *EGA,* or *Enhanced Graphics Adapter,* appeared in 1984 and boosted color graphics up to 16 simultaneous colors at CGA's resolution. Later models sported memory chips and were capable of 16 colors out of a *palette* (color range) of 64, at 640 by 350 resolution. You can still find EGA monitors and cards on the market. For those on a budget who don't need to run the graphics-demanding Windows or other GUI software, EGA is a decent first standard.

VGA

Chances are, you'll buy a card from the *Video Graphics Array*, or *VGA* standard. Out of a palette of 262,144 colors, you get either 256 simultaneously, at 320 by 200 resolution, or 16 at full 640 by 480 resolution. Most preconfigured PCs come bundled with VGA monitors, with VGA cards already stuck inside the system box. Most of today's software packages take advantage of the VGA standard, which at some resolutions can reach near-photographic quality.

Super VGA

Super VGA offers all the colors of VGA but at an even higher resolution, 800 by 600 pixels. Also known as *Extended VGA* or *VGA Plus*, this standard isn't standard enough. That's why different SVGA cards must offer their own, specific software instructions, called *drivers*, to let your PC know you have SVGA graphics.

Check your software's requirements for any specific SVGA card brand name.

The 8514/A Standard

Also known as *Hi-Res SVGA*, this standard offers a tightly focused 1,024 by 768 display, 512K of video memory, and a graphics coprocessor chip that hastens drawing. Monitors supporting this standard are up there in the price range, but they'll start becoming more affordable soon. Software, too, is only starting to come around to this level of graphics quality.

You'll pay more for video cards that offer the most colors at the highest resolutions. At the time of this writing, only a few high-end graphics packages support the highest Super VGA modes. As you know by now, it's best to take your software's requirements into consideration when choosing any component in your PC system: especially a monitor/ video card combination.

BOTTOM LINE

Resolution vs. Color

No matter how far PC graphics have come, users still face the same dilemma as in the old HGC/CGA days: resolution vs. color. That's why the typical ad describing a VGA card reads: "640 x 480 at 16 colors, or 320 x 200 at 256 colors." With cards, there's always the trade-off between less colors at a higher resolution, or more colors and a fuzzier picture. Table 13.1. shows the evolution of resolutions and colors offered by different monitor/video card combinations.

Table 13.1   Video cards differ in the resolution and number of colors they offer.

Graphics Standard	Colors	Resolution
MDA	single (text only)	720 x 350
CGA	4	320 x 200
	2	640 x 200
HGC	monochrome	720 x 348
EGA	16	640 x 350
VGA	16	640 x 480
	256	320 x 200
SVGA*	16	800 x 600
8514/A	256	1,024 x 768

*Note: SVGA, not being a true standard, varies in its capabilities from brand to brand.

Video Cards Need Memory, Too

Graphics cards fly when equipped with memory chips, which take the graphics processing load off the main processor and speed up the rate at which graphics display and screens refresh.

Typically, you'll see a card advertised with 256K or 512K of RAM, although some cards hold several megabytes of video RAM. Check out Table 13.2 to see what different levels RAM offers. You'll pay extra for more RAM, but it may be worth it for your graphics-intensive applications, or if you plan to run a lot of Windows programs.

Find out how much memory a card comes with, and also what the card's maximum memory capacity is. You may want to upgrade later. Figure 13.2 shows where memory is located on a video card.

Fill a card with as much RAM as you can afford. Upgrading is a pain.

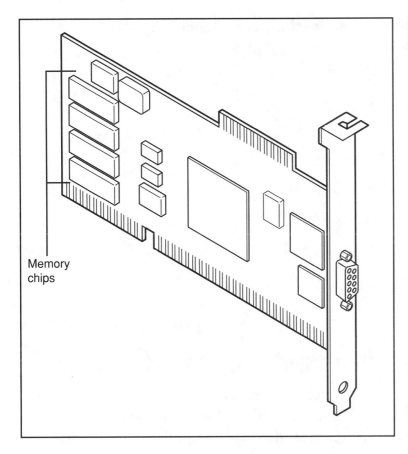

Memory
chips

Figure 13.2

Check the video card's on-board RAM, as well as spare RAM slots for future upgrades.

Jär-gen:

The type of memory chips makes a difference in a card's speed. DRAM chips, also known as Dynamic RAM, are slower than special VRAM, or Video RAM chips. But cards with VRAM cost more.

Table 13.2   Approximate performance depending on video card memory.

Memory	Resolution	Colors
256K	640 x 480	16
	800 x 600	16
512K	640 x 480	256
	800 x 600	256
	1,024 x 768	16
1MB	1,024 x 768	256
	1,280 x 1,024	16

What's a Bit Number Doing on the Card?

Chapter 7 discusses how a PC motherboard's expansion slots differ in size, or bit width. Recall that a bit is the name for the smallest unit data can be broken down into. Video cards also differ in bit widths. As with other types of expansion cards, higher bit widths ensure that information can travel at a higher rate through the card. Because graphics can really bog down a PC, if you'll be doing lots, invest in a video card with a higher bit width.

An altogether different "bit number" exists with video cards (just to confuse shoppers). If you see "4-bit color" in a video card ad, this refers to the number of bits it takes for the screen to show pixels. This is extremely technical, so for now, know that the higher the " -bit color" number, the more colors and the more expensive the card! Currently, the high-end cards run up to 24 bits, enabling 16-million-plus possible colors. That's neat . . . except that most software can't take advantage of it!

Video Accelerator Boards

Video accelerator boards replace a PC's video card to enable souped-up graphics capabilities, thanks to on-board graphics coprocessors and, often, VRAM video memory chips. Video accelerator boards should offer a 1,280 by 1,024 resolution, in non-interlaced mode, with refresh rates of 70Hz or higher to reduce flicker. These boards typically come in 32-bit widths, as Figure 13.3 shows.

Video accelerator boards differ from local bus video boards, another way to improve a PC's graphics capability. A PC system with a local bus has moved the video circuitry from a card in the expansion slot

Jär-gen:

What's the Ad Mean by VESA?   VESA stands for Video Electronics Standards Association, a group of companies who set standards for video cards and monitors. A card touted as VESA-standard means its manufacturer complies with VESA's specifications. The VESA folks are working on a standard meant to speed up image loading. Creating a standard should ensure that different manufacturers' local bus video cards can fit into any brand of motherboard.

directly onto the motherboard, so it's connected right to the CPU, or the local bus, rather than the expansion bus.

Although local bus video can load images quickly into video memory, they still place the video grunt work on the CPU's shoulders. For now, the video accelerator meets the advanced user's needs best.

Figure 13.3

Video accelerator boards soup up a PC's graphics capabilities.

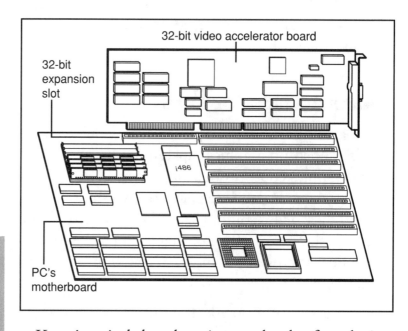

Only users with intense graphics requirements should seek out accelerator boards—they're costly and often slow down in plain VGA mode.

BOTTOM LINE

Keep in mind that these intense levels of resolution can cram too much detail onto a smaller monitor. Consider going all the way to a 20-inch screen if your graphics requirements demand a video accelerator. Talk to users and jot down their experiences with the different brands. Read reviews in magazines, too.

Which Video Card Should I Buy?

Look at different card/monitor combinations in stores. See what your planned software requires, and try out a couple of the applications with the video card.

Get a monitor that matches the capability of your video card. Make sure the two are compatible in areas like non-interlacing, multi-frequency modes and vertical scan rates, covered in Chapter 12.

If you buy a multi-frequency monitor, make sure the card enables mode-switching through software, instead of your having to fiddle with dip switches on the card whenever you want to change modes.

In This Chapter, You Learned . . .

Video cards inside the PC drive the monitor. The display's quality represents the combined capabilities of the monitor, video card, and software you're running.

> *The best card for your money is a 16-bit Super VGA card with at least 512K memory and a money-back guarantee. If you get Super VGA, make sure the video card comes with a disk of software drivers to run your planned applications—or else you'll see them in plain VGA-mode.*
>
> **BOTTOM LINE**

Color and resolution put heavy loads on the PC, so you may have to strike a compromise in your applications. For truly intensive graphics, you may want to investigate graphics accelerator boards, often called Windows accelerators.

Chapter 13 Checklist:

Brand: _____

Model #: _____

Resolution Modes: _____

Pixels: _____

Colors: _____

Total Palette: _____

Memory: _____

Bit-Width: _____

Price: _____

Don't Forget to Ask . . .

- How many resolution modes can the card produce?

- Will my planned software work with the card?

- Will the card support the monitor I like?

- If my monitor supports it, can the card adapt to older video modes like EGA or monochrome graphics?

- How much memory is included?

- Does the card sport local bus technology?

- Are the card's vertical scanning rate and non-interlacing (or interlacing) compatible with the monitor I like?

- How many colors will the card display?

- Would my application run better with a graphics accelerator card?

Notes: _____

_____

_____

_____

_____

Keyboards

A keyboard helps you put information into the PC where it can do some good. A keyboard's not as glamorous as a monitor, to be sure, but it's just as essential to get one you like. You'll be looking at the monitor you choose for hours on end—and you'll be tapping your keyboard for just as many hours.

Aren't All Keyboards the Same?

A computer's keyboard is based on a typewriter keyboard, with some extra keys for some computer chores. The keyboard connects to a special port in the back of your computer.

Keyboards come in different styles of two basic models, but beyond that, they all seem to *feel* different. Some people like a keyboard with a little resistance to it. Others prefer a "loose" keyboard that performs at the slightest tap.

> *Keyboards made by the Compaq company are notoriously firm. And people still rave about the touch on the original IBM keyboard.*

You can't enjoy your computer as long as you hate the feel of your keyboard, so try out a few different brands. Mail-order shoppers will have to try some out at a store, then ask some very detailed questions over the phone! You might buy one that feels exactly like the one you use at work—or one that's just the opposite!

Standard or Enhanced Keyboard?

One of the keys used most often on a PC is the Enter key. It works like a typewriter's carriage return (in word processing) and sends instructions of every type to the PC.

Ninety-nine percent of all PC systems come with a keyboard already included, or bundled. Even so, if you decide you don't like its feel, leave the keyboard at the store and buy one you prefer. The dealer can usually be talked into a small price reduction for a system without a keyboard.

BOTTOM LINE

Original

Standard

Enhanced

Figure 14.1

Original IBM PC, standard, and enhanced keyboards.

Jär-gen:

Keyboards come in two basic models, standard and enhanced. Check out the differences in the keyboards Figure 14.1 shows. You'll find plenty of variations within these divisions. Both models are vast improvements over the original IBM PC keyboard, which, although it felt great, had no labels on its Shift, Tab, or Backspace keys!

ISTORY

The original IBM PC keyboard sported such a small *Enter* key that users often accidentally hit the Print-Screen key instead. If they slipped and tapped the adjacent Shift key, too, the PC immediately sent their screen's contents to the printer.

The Standard Keyboard

Like the keyboard on the original IBM PC, the standard keyboard lines up the *function keys* used in working with a software program along the left side. This keyboard improved upon the original keyboard by labeling the Tab and Shift keys and by beefing up the Enter key size. Standard keyboards come in two versions: an *XT-compatible model* and an *AT-compatible model.*

NOTE

If you have an older computer (below a 286), it's important that you get an XT-compatible keyboard; an AT-compatible keyboard will not work. Conversely, if you have a 286 or above (an AT computer), make sure you get an AT-compatible keyboard.

The 101-Key Enhanced Keyboard

One big difference between the standard and enhanced models is the function key placement. They've been moved from the left side to a row along the top, above the number keys and far out of reach of most touch-typists. (Not an enhancement in my book!)

**ISTORY**

Northgate brand keyboards were the first to offer enhanced keyboards with function keys in both spots, so people didn't have to relearn typing inside their favorite software just because they got a new keyboard. (Many bought Northgate computers just for the keyboard.)

Also, enhanced keyboards offer a bank of *cursor movement keys* separate from the *numeric keypad*. *Cursor keys* let you move the typing point, or *cursor*, around the screen. A numeric keypad works as a calculator to perform operations on numbers. Standard keyboard users press a *NumLock* key to toggle between cursor or numeric keypad modes, so they can't simultaneously work with numbers and move their cursor around—a big hassle for regular spreadsheet users. The enhanced keyboard is a big improvement over the standard keyboard's combined numeric keypad/cursor keys. Look back at Figure 14.1 to compare them.

Another Alternative: The Dvorak Keyboard

The original typewriter layout was designed to befuddle speedy typists enough to keep the old mechanical keys from jamming. Today's electronic keyboard poses no such pitfalls for users with agile fingers. You can overcome this interesting remnant of the machine age by buying a Dvorak keyboard, like the one in Figure 14.2. It's specially designed to take advantage of the stronger fingers on the right hand. To avoid confusion, make sure keyboards you use elsewhere are of the same layout.

Figure 14.2

If you'd like to type faster, the Dvorak keyboard optimizes every stroke.

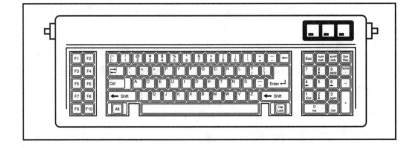

Built-In Trackballs and Other Keyboard Extras

Keyboards, once simple and predictable, are gaining in features and in cost. You can buy a model with a built-in trackball device that lets you position the cursor by rolling your fingertips instead of pecking at the cursor keys, as Figure 14.3 shows. Trackballs, like mice in Chapter 15, speed your movements in graphics applications.

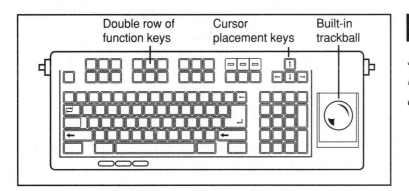

Figure 14.3

Some keyboards come with built-in trackballs to ease cursor placement.

Other keyboard models sport built-in calculators and even rubbery touch-pads to replace the numeric keypad. Many new models offer a row of programmable function keys along the top. These let you record keystrokes you find yourself repeating often. You assign the sequence to one of these keys and then press the one key instead of several. Imagine typing your name and address with a single keystroke.

These high-end keyboard features sport high-end price tags, so be careful to assess what features you'll truly need.

Wrist Protectors

On a long-term basis, the repeated motion of typing can cause a range of painful conditions to hands and wrists. Fortunately, most computer stores and mail-order companies carry products that ease the blows. A keyboard wrist protector, a thick strip of rubbery wet suit material, may be all you need to cushion the impact from hours of typing.

Keyboard Covers

Clear plastic devices on the market sit over your keyboard and protect it from dust, crumbs, and even beverage spills, while still allowing you to type. Some find typing atop one of these devices just as easy as without—it's one of those things you have to try out before you buy.

Keycaps

Most software enables you to reassign keys and their functions in that program. Special plastic key caps fit over normal keys on the keyboard and give you a way to label the reassigned keys, as Figure 14.4 shows. Colored keycaps let you color-code frequently used functions.

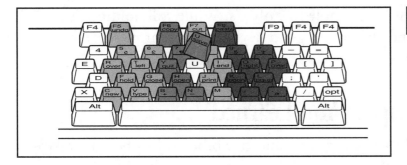

Figure 14.4

Keycaps provide a way to customize a keyboard.

Pre-Purchase Keyboard Tests to Perform

When shopping for a keyboard, check for the position of most frequently used keys such as Enter, Backspace, the Shift keys, and the Function keys. Make sure they're in the right place for you—you'll be pressing them a lot.

Test the keyboard's ergonomic-awareness by seeing if you can raise or lower its back end to a better angle. Sit down and type a few paragraphs on a variety of different keyboards to see how the "touch" appeals to you.

Check the keyboard's fitness with the trusty *N-key rollover test.* A quality keyboard should let you strike another key while holding down the first one and making it repeat. To test the keyboard, press down the "j" key and make a whole row of "j"s. While still holding down "j", press "f", "g", and "h", too. A good keyboard will throw something besides "j"s on the screen.

In This Chapter, You Learned . . .

Finding the right keyboard is a subjective process. Just because a keyboard comes bundled with a PC doesn't mean you have to take it home. Try out a range of models and buy the one that feels right. Function-key placement and the general keyboard layout should suit you.

Chapter 14 Checklist:

Keyboard Brand Tested: _____

Look: _____

Feel: _____

Enter-key Accessibility: _____

Price: _____

Don't Forget to Ask . . .

- Is it compatible with your PC model?
- Does your work involve heavy number crunching or otherwise call for a separate numeric keypad?
- Can you adjust the keyboard's angle for comfort?
- Have you tried out a wrist protector?

Notes: _____

_____

_____

_____

_____

_____

_____

_____

_____

_____

_____

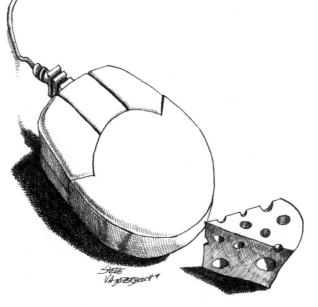

The Computer Mouse and Other Input Devices

Despite the cute name, a computer mouse can boost your efficiency in a decidedly no-nonsense way. Like the keyboards described in the last chapter, a mouse is an *input device*. Positioning the cursor with a mouse gives you another way of telling the PC to do something. Paired with a keyboard, a computer mouse gives you quick, smooth control over your applications.

Although a mouse is the most common of its genre, a range of input devices exist. Mouse pens, joysticks, hand scanners, and trackballs each give a measure of control to users involved in more specialized applications.

But a Mouse Is a Furry Rodent, Right?

A mouse (see Figure 15.1) is an input device that moves a pointer on your PC's monitor. White and shaped like a bar of Dove soap, the computer mouse has one, two, or three buttons along the back, and a ball in its underbelly. The tail-like mouse cord connects to the PC's serial or mouse port. The whole effect, with the "tail" cord, the white shape, and the buttons, looks like a mouse. (Okay, so computer designers *have* been sitting too long in front of their PCs!)

Figure 15.1

It's a bar of soap, it's a plane . . . it's a mouse?

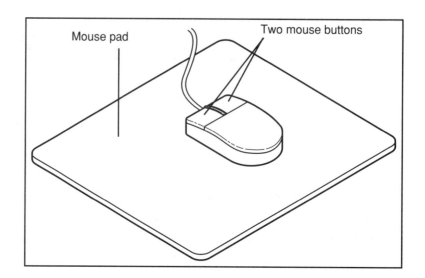

Mouse pad

Two mouse buttons

HISTORY

Neanderthal Mouse Back in 1967, a researcher came up with the mouse prototype while working on ways to make computers more understandable and easier to use. Softball-sized, the device had three control buttons where eyes and mouth belonged, plus large wheels underneath for "feet." Embellished with a tail-like cord, the device was quickly dubbed "mouse." The name stuck.

How Does It Work?

You place your hand atop the mouse and roll it around over a mouse pad, pressing buttons along the back, as your software requires. As the mouse rolls up and down, across and back, the cursor on screen scuttles around correspondingly—pushed by a signal that reads the mouse motion.

In some software applications, the mouse pointer looks like an arrow; in others, a bar, as Figure 15.2 shows. When you maneuver the mouse pointer to a desired object on screen, whether it's a block of text, a cell in a spreadsheet, or a command box in Windows, you hold down a mouse button to *select*, or highlight text. You can press-and-release, or *click* (even *double-click*) the button to activate a software command.

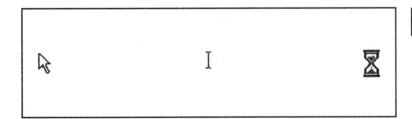

Figure 15.2

A mouse pointer assumes various shapes on-screen, depending on the software you're using.

Not all software supports a mouse. If it does, you can use the mouse's pointer instead of tedious cursor keys to highlight text, invoke commands, view menus, drag objects, and navigate around the program.

Who Needs a Mouse or Other Input Devices?

- *Windows Users*   Although Windows and other GUI programs come with keyboard commands, forget it! You need a mouse if you plan to run Windows and Windows-like programs. Period.

- *Desktop Publishers*   Designers wouldn't think of trying to navigate their software without a mouse. Dragging and sizing images, making subtle text adjustments, creating type styles: a mouse improves all these functions. Many desktop publishers opt for a trackball, instead. Scanners help these professionals add graphics to their work.

- *Computer Artists and Multimedia Producers*   Mouse pens, scanners, and mice ease the production of computer art and multimedia efforts.

- *Accountants and Business Professionals*   Mice make even the most ho-hum business applications zing. Once you select a spreadsheet's rows and columns with a mouse you will never go without again.

Mouse Comparisons

The mouse family is sizable, with many sub-species. Whether country mouse or city mouse, an easy way to compare them is by *ppi*, or *points per inch* resolution. A ppi of 200 lets you select objects more precisely; 400 ppi requires even less wrist motion to move the pointer across the screen.

Two Interfaces: Bus Mouse or Serial Mouse

A serial mouse connects to a PC's serial port. A bus mouse comes with an expansion card, or the PC may already come with a "mouse" port. (If you forgot ports, head back to Chapter 9.) The type you buy depends on which slot is free on your PC. If your computer is long on expansion slots, buy a bus mouse. If you have few free slots but you do have a free serial port, your best buy's a serial mouse.

Bus mice cost a bit more; some users report more responsiveness and better circuitry within. Plus they don't take up one of your serial ports, which could be better filled by a modem (discussed in Chapter 17).

Optical Mouse vs. Mechanical Mouse

All mice glide around on a rubbery, cushiony mouse pad. But an optical mouse sports optical sensors that "read" a special pad printed with an optically detectable grid. The higher-priced optical mouse offers increased precision over the mechanical mouse which works by means of a roller ball that can clog up with dirt or lint.

Some computer stores stock special mouse-ball cleaning kits to keep your mouse preened to perfection.

The Cordless Mouse

Cordless mice come in two species: *radio-controlled* and *infrared*. Both types liberate you from a mouse cord, since they work via a receiving unit, which connects to the PC via a serial port or expansion slot. The cordless mouse shoots out waves recording its position back to the unit, which in turn communicates to the PC. Check out Figure 15.3.

The radio mouse costs more than the infrared—both cost more than a normal mouse. The required mechanics lead to a larger-than-normal mouse which some users say is too big to grasp comfortably. The infrared model works fine until an object like a coffee cup is inadvertently placed between the mouse and its receiving unit. Then the beam is blocked and mousing ceases.

Wait until the novelty of your new PC has worn off before buying one of these toys, even if they do unleash you from the mouse-strings.

Mini Mouse

Where's Mickey? A tiny, 2 1/4-inch mouse called the Gulliver hopes to take mousing to new levels of portability. Held with two fingers, like a piece of chalk, the Gulliver works with a friction-activated, floating-ball movement that lets a user mouse around anywhere, even on the sleeve of a jacket.

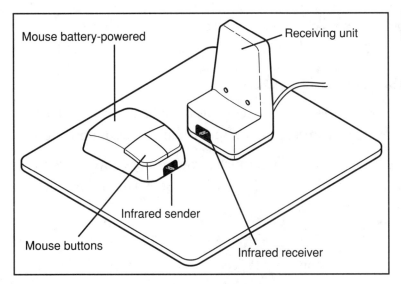

Figure 15.3

Cordless mice beam their location to a receiving unit.

What's Mouse Compatibility?

Most software supports a variety of mouse types, but there are certain standards in the industry for which many manufacturers follow. Microsoft-compatible is the most common standard; Logitech-compatible is another.

Why Do Some Models Have Three Buttons?

Mice that are *Microsoft-compatible* have two buttons, while mice that are *Logitech-compatible* have three. Very few software packages allow you to use the third (middle) button. Windows itself recognizes only one mouse button, but some Windows applications allow you to use two or even three buttons.

What Mouse Should I Buy?

Although many users recommend a bus mouse over a serial model, I've never seen much difference. Buy whatever mouse your system can accommodate.

Look for a mouse with a 200 points per inch resolution or above. As with keyboards, mice are a matter of comfort and usability, so make sure you buy one with a money-back guarantee.

Whatever you buy, make sure it's Microsoft-compatible.

The mouse you buy should come with special software, called a device driver. This software tells your PC that you have a mouse by putting a line in one of two crucial files in your PC, either CONFIG.SYS or AUTOEXEC.BAT. Have a techie friend help you install your mouse, or ask nicely at the local user group. If all else fails, a good DOS book should help, like *At Home with MS-DOS* by Paul McFedries.

Often, a mouse's software includes special menu or graphics programs. It's fun to play with your mouse's graphics program, especially if you have a color monitor.

Other Input Devices

Portable and laptop computers have spawned a nest of mouse substitutes. When shopping for one of these pointing devices, make sure it comes with a Microsoft-compatible mouse driver. It's essential to look at connectors: If it requires a serial port, do you have a spare? If it requires an expansion slot, do you have an extra one? Make sure the cord's not too long . . . or too short! No matter how small the ball is in one of these devices, make sure it moves freely and feels right.

Trackball

Take a mouse and (very gently!) flip it on its back. Now roll the mouse ball around with your fingertips. Voilà! That's the basic idea behind a trackball—all that's left is to pry the mouse buttons off the bottom and glue them on either side of the ball. (Do not try this at home.)

> *Some people enjoy the feel of a trackball, and others prefer a mouse, so this is another one of those decisions you must make by testing the alternatives.*
>
> **BOTTOM LINE**

You can buy trackballs attached to high-end keyboards, as you read in Chapter 14. They're also available in stand-alone models that sit next to your keyboard, where a mouse and mousepad would be. Trackballs are mouse balls on steroids; most average about the size of an eight ball. Miniature trackball units clip onto the side of a desktop or laptop keyboard, as Figure 15.4 shows.

The advantage to trackballs is that, being stationary, they take up less desk room.

Figure 15.4

Miniature trackballs attach to a keyboard or a portable PC.

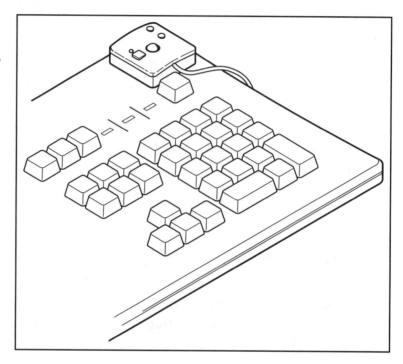

Mouse Pen

Imagine a pen with a mouse's rolling ball where the ball-point tip should be. Now feed the pen a steady diet of coconut ice cream and cheesecake so it bulges into behemoth stage. Stick some miniaturized mouse buttons down the front and you've just imagined a mouse pen (see Figure 15.5). Mouse pens are a perfect choice for people who want the agility, but not the bulk, of a true mouse.

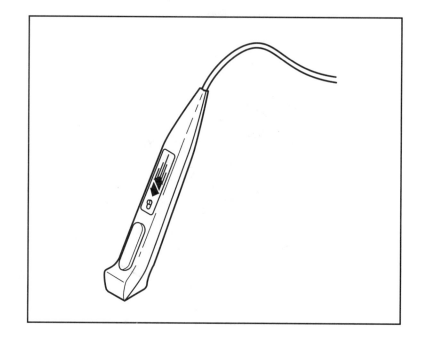

Figure 15.5

Mouse pens present a compact alternative to mice.

Scanners, Joysticks, and Other Input Toys

Besides the mouse family, there are many other input devices on the market. Some are more practical than others. As with any computer add-on, check to see what your software requires before you buy.

Hand-Held Scanners

A hand-held scanner lets you put pictures into your PC, ready to be added to a newsletter or transformed into Windows wallpaper. You hold down the scanner and guide it over the image to be scanned, as Figure 15.6 shows, kind of like the bar-code scanner at the grocery checkout counter.

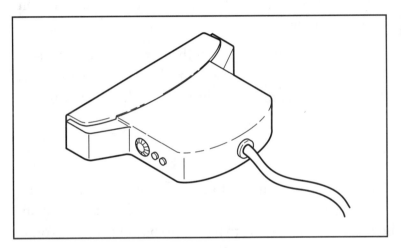

Figure 15.6

Scanners transform pictures into information your PC can process.

> *If you need super-high resolution, investigate the next level, called flatbed scanners, which work like a copy machine. Scanners range in price from $150 to several thousand dollars, so read reviews and become familiar with leading brands and their features before you buy.*

BOTTOM LINE

The wider the scanner, the wider the picture it scans. Most can scan either a half-page (4 inches) or a full-page width (8 inches). Special software lets you "stitch" the strips together to form a complete picture. More expensive scanners can also handle text, when teamed with optical character recognition software. Imagine being able to scan a document into your word processor instead of typing it.

Hand-held scanners vary in their image quality, measured in a type of resolution termed *dots per inch* (*dpi*). As with monitors and printers in the next chapter, sharper output costs more money.

Joysticks

Joysticks sport a padded, upright arm similar to the controls on video arcade games. They connect to a "game" port on a PC system. Joysticks can move up, down, right, left, and diagonally, and sport two or three buttons that let you blast Klingons with aplomb. Did I say "blast Klingons?" Sadly, joysticks are used for little more than computer games. But what a difference a good joystick makes. This is another one to test out for the right feel.

Flight Yoke

Flight simulators rank among the best-selling software programs. An inventive company markets a special device tailored to the many flight-simulator fans, called the Maxx Yoke. The Yoke looks just like an airplane's steering mechanism, or yoke, complete with optional foot pedals. The steering wheel even slides toward and away from the "pilot" to add an extra air of realism to the in-flight experience.

In This Chapter, You Learned . . .

Mice, trackballs, and the more offbeat input devices team up with a PC's keyboard to enhance your control over software applications. Computer gamers wield joysticks to demolish asteroids, or simply to navigate the screens of an adventure game. Scanners help you embellish your work with pictures, or even input text.

Chapter 15 Checklist:

- Does my software call for a mouse? Will it even support one?

- Have I tested how the mice feel? Priced serial and bus versions? Optical and mechanical?

- Do I have the right connectors? A spare slot, or serial port?

- Does the mouse come with mouse drivers? A menu or graphics program?

- Have I remembered a mouse pad?

- Would a trackball work better? A mouse pen or other pointing device?

Notes: _____

_____

_____

_____

_____

_____

_____

_____

_____

_____

_____

_____

_____

_____

_____

_____

_____

_____

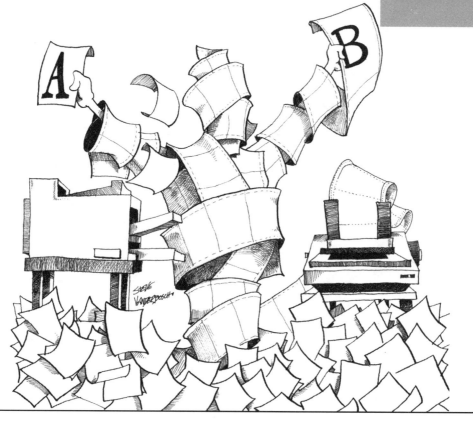

Printers

By now, you've gained an appreciation for how hard the PC's components work together to accomplish your tasks. You've worked hard, too, learning about PC hardware and how to choose the best components for your needs. You have more work in front of you, as you learn your operating system, your software, and—as time passes—discover even more about your hardware.

Wouldn't it be neat if there were a way to show off all this hard work? There is, once you buy a printer for your PC. A printer provides a way for you and your PC to produce printouts, or *hard copy*, so you can proudly share your hard-won efforts with the rest of the world.

This chapter describes several printer families. Within each family lies a range of choices to ensure that you find an efficient, cost-effective printing solution.

Let's Begin with General Advice . . .

As you're looking at various printers, keep in mind these things:

- Some printers have both *parallel* and *serial interfaces* (that is, they're capable of hooking into either a parallel or a serial port on your PC). Some printers are capable of only one or the other. Parallel is faster, but the printer must be within about 10 feet of the PC. Serial is slower but the cable can be much longer.

- Some printers work with several computer brands, like Apple Macintoshes, for example. If you're interested in one of these, find out up front if it will work with your PC.

- Printer cables (the cables that connect your parallel or serial port to the printer) are sold separately; make sure you buy the appropriate cable. Ask the salesperson for help in selecting one.

- If you're buying a less-popular brand of printer (that is, a printer other than an Epson or Hewlett Packard), make sure your software will support the printer. Many off-brand printers can emulate (imitate) a popular model to work with your software.

Jär-gen:

Dot-matrix printers come in 9-pin and 24-pin versions. They get their name from the number of pins (either 9 or 24) arranged in a matrix inside their print heads. When the print head strikes against a ribbon and onto paper, the pins scramble to form the letter, number, or symbol needed. Each pin of the matrix adds a dot to the character image.

Dot-Matrix Printers: The No-Frills Standard

Dot-matrix printers offer decent text and graphics output—and even color, with the right ribbons—at a reasonable price. That's why computer stores sell more of these printers than any other type.

Dot Matrix Resolution

There's that word *resolution* again! Printers, like many other computer accessories, measure their graphics quality in resolutions of dots per inch, or dpi, where higher dpi rates ensure sharper print quality.

Because more dots make up each character, 24 pins produce a finer character than nine, as Figure 16.1 shows. Accordingly, a 24-pin dot-matrix printer usually costs two or three times as much as the 9-pin variety.

BOTTOM LINE

24-pin output   9-pin output

```
Before you can run any program, you have to boot your computer.
Boot is a fancy term that means you have to turn on your computer
with the disk operating system files in place: the files have to
be on your computer's hard disk (if it has one) or on a floppy
disk that is in one of the floppy disk drives.

     Before you can run any program, you have to boot your
computer. Boot is a fancy term that means you have to turn on
your computer with the disk operating system files in place: the
files have to be on your computer's hard disk (if it has one) or
on a floppy disk that is in one of the floppy disk drives.
```

Figure 16.1

A 24-pin dot-matrix printer produces a sharper image than a 9-pin model.

Although 9-pin dot-matrix printers sport a switch that jumps to "near-letter quality" mode, the result leaves something to be desired.

243

The print heads on the 9-pin models try to top their personal best by making several passes over each dot. Though darker, the result does not exactly epitomize high resolution, as Figure 16.2 shows.

Draft mode output | Near-letter quality output

```
        Before you can run any program, you have to boot your
computer. Boot is a fancy term that means you have to turn on
your computer with the disk operating system files in place:  the
files have to be on your computer's hard disk (if it has one) or
on a floppy disk that is in one of the floppy disk drives.

        Before you can run any program, you have to boot your
computer. Boot is a fancy term that means you have to turn on
your computer with the disk operating system files in place:  the
files have to be on your computer's hard disk (if it has one) or
on a floppy disk that is in one of the floppy disk drives.
```

Figure 16.2

Draft mode and near-letter quality mode from a 9-pin dot-matrix printer.

Jär-gen:

A business letter needs to look as spiffy as possible. That's why the highest ranking printers tout their ability to spit out letter-quality documents. The term near-letter quality, or NLQ, evolved when marketing types needed a way to say their printers were almost capable of letter quality output.

The 24-pin models can print great-looking letters. But laser and inkjet printers—and older daisywheel models, the original letter-quality printers—leave dot-matrix in the dust.

Dot Matrix Speed

Dot-matrix printers race along anywhere from 30 cps for a 9-pin model in NLQ mode to 430 cps for the newest 24-pin models in draft mode. Some of the high-end models offer *quiet mode*, at the expense of speed.

Dot-matrix printers' speeds are measured in cps, or characters per second. The higher the cps, the faster the print job. Because ads broadcast only the biggest numbers, many brag about the printer's speed while printing draft mode, a faster, lesser quality printing mode good for printing first drafts. Ask what the model clocks in LQ (letter-quality) or NLQ (near letter-quality) mode, especially if you'll be using these high-quality modes consistently.

Dot Matrix Noise Levels

Dot-matrix printers belong to the *impact printer* family. This means the print head bangs (loudly) against the print carriage. After half a page or so of printing takes place, you'll begin to see why *non-impact printers*, like the laser printers discussed further down, are so popular. Dot-matrix printers often sport pause buttons that let you interrupt the print job long enough to talk on the phone, and then resume.

Impact printers do have an advantage: They print well on multipart forms, where you must bear down on the top page hard enough to leave an impression on the pages underneath.

Dot Matrix Extras

The more expensive 24-pin models offer extra plastic noise shields.

They also may sport wider carriages that accept paper up to 14 inches in width, as Figure 16.3 shows. Also dubbed 132-column printers, these wide-carriage models offer more versatility in typing odd-sized forms than their 80-column wide, standard siblings.

Other Dot Matrix Printer Options

Most dot matrix printers provide attachments that accommodate *continuous-feed*, or *tractor-feed*, paper. That way, you don't have to feed in each individual sheet—the paper automatically advances and feeds through.

A printer with easy-to-use controls on the front will make adjustments easier for you; avoid printers that force you to open a panel and flip switches to make simple changes.

Many models offer various type styles, or *fonts*, built-in. These fonts come in handy when you're working with a software package that relies on your printer's fonts, such as WordPerfect. If you're using software with its own fonts, such as Windows 3.1, you'll probably never use a printer's built-in fonts.

Most printers also come with a small *print buffer*. A print buffer is a small amount of RAM in the printer (8K is common) that holds data until the print head catches up. You can pay extra for larger print buffers, but there's little reason to with a dot matrix printer. (Printer RAM is very important with laser printers, however.)

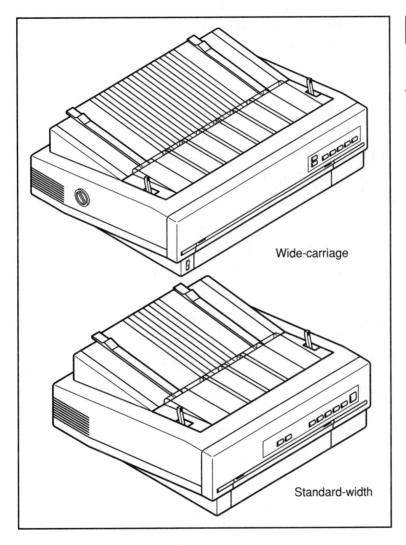

> *If you have a limited amount of money to spend, forego color in favor of better black-and-white print quality.*

BOTTOM LINE

And finally, some dot matrix printers offer color output. The quality of dot matrix color printing often leaves something to be desired, especially on complex images, but it's fun, especially for families with children.

Is Dot-Matrix for You?

Dot-matrix printers are noisy. But they offer decent print quality and versatility—including multipart and extra-wide form printing—unmatched by the other printer families.

In general, look for the highest resolution at the lowest price, with the features that are important to you. If you need an inexpensive, simple printer next to your PC for drafts and quick, almost-near-letter quality printouts, buy a 9-pin dot matrix printer. High-volume users and small businesses may opt for a 24-pin model, still a versatile, affordable printer solution.

Count on paying about $150 for an average 9-pin model. A good 24-pin model runs about $300, and you can pay up to $800 for a high-end model that prints multipart forms.

Laser Printers

A *laser printer* works similar to a copy machine. It quickly and quietly produces high-quality text and graphic printouts. A million amateur desktop publishers were born the day laser printers appeared on the scene.

Laser is the most expensive printer type on the market, costing as much as a mid-range 386 PC. But if your needs include large print jobs, high-quality graphics, a mixture of type styles, or just intensely great print quality, look at a laser printer.

Laser Resolution

Laser printer output quality rates in dots per inch, or dpi. Most models on the market offer up to 300 dpi. As with other devices, higher dpi means a sharper looking printout. Graphics are affected by dpi more than text (see Figure 16.4).

There are some fancy high-resolution laser printers on the market that offer up to 1,000 dpi. Of course, their prices aren't in the range of most home users' budgets.

Figure 16.4

Laser printout graphics quality improves as dpi increases.

This is printed at 75 dpi.

This is printed at 150 dpi.

This is printed at 300 dpi.

Laser Fonts

Laser printers typically come with several fonts, as shown in Figure 16.5, from as few as 15 to as many as 50.

Fifty fonts seem like a lot, but each type size is considered a separate font, as well as each combination of attributes. For example, 12-point Courier is a font, 12-point bold Courier is another, and 14-point bold italic Courier is another. In reality, a printer with 50 fonts may only offer 3 or 4 type styles.

You can spice up documents and fliers with different fonts in two ways: through font cartridges and downloadable fonts. Although faster, font cartridges cost more than the many software fonts, also called *downloadable* fonts, available free (or very cheap) from various sources.

Software often comes with downloadable fonts too; CorelDRAW! 3.0, for example, comes with over 100 different Windows 3.1-compatible type styles.

Figure 16.5

Fonts entertain the eye and make your message more effective.

In the beginning...

Call me Ishmael

My dearest darling:

APPROVED 8/5/92

Big Clearance Sale!

Laser Speed

Laser printers clock output in *ppm*, or *pages per minute*, averaging about 6 ppm. That number refers to the printer's maximum speed; if you're printing graphics or special fonts, it'll take longer.

Laser Memory

Laser printers sport their own memory chips to speed the printing process. Low-end laser printers come with 512K of RAM standard, which is not enough to print a full-page graphic image. Buy as much extra RAM for your printer as you can afford, at least 2MB or more if your applications require mixing a variety of type styles on one page.

Laser Maintenance/Supply Costs

Besides the expensive initial price, laser printers tally high upkeep costs to replace toner cartridges and other consumables.

When shopping, find out if the toner cartridge, developer, and drum are one unit, or come separately. Ask how much each replacement component costs, and how long each one lasts. Combination units usually cost more to replace, but they don't have to be replaced as often.

PostScript Emulation

PostScript capabilities can boost a printer's cost significantly, as much as $1,000. Some printers offer PostScript emulation (imitation) at a reduced cost. It's best to see what your software requires before springing for this sophisticated extra. Most home users will not benefit enough from PostScript to justify the extra cost.

Jär-gen:

Once you start looking at laser printers, you'll find the word PostScript cropping up repeatedly. PostScript is a page-description language built into some printers to improve the way the PC and the computer communicate. PostScript printers include 17 or 35 scalable fonts (fonts that will print in any size) and give you the ability to print Encapsulated PostScript (EPS) graphics files.

ISTORY

For many years, PostScript was prized for its scalable fonts. As you learned in the Laser Fonts discussion, a font cartridge stores each size of each typeface with each attribute (like bold or italic) as a separate entity. PostScript printers, on the other hand, sported built-in fonts which the printer could print at any size "on demand." Users of PostScript printers were not slaves to cartridges and downloadable fonts—all the fonts they needed were stored neatly inside the printer's memory!

When Microsoft introduced Windows 3.1, however, a new technology called TrueType entered the market. TrueType fonts are stored in the computer, like downloadable fonts, but they're scalable like the PostScript fonts, so each typeface can be printed in any size. Because TrueType fonts don't take up very much hard disk space, a Windows 3.1 user can have hundreds of scalable typefaces—instead of just 17 or 35—available all the time.

TrueType did not give Windows 3.1 users the ability to print Encapsulated PostScript graphics files, however, and PostScript is still the language of choice among most professional desktop publishers, because it was the standard for so long.

Laser Printer Summary

Quiet, high-resolution printouts at a speedy pace can be yours with a laser printer, but at a price. Expect to pay at least $500 for a rock-bottom model. PostScript compatibles start at $1,500, and soar way up there, depending on output speed and resolution, among other factors. This family of printers is quickly becoming the small-business standard.

Other Printers

A variety of other printers round out this large family of computer peripherals.

Inkjet Printers

Printers from this family form characters in dots, like those of the dot-matrix family. These non-impact printers shoot blobs of ink instead of striking the printer carriage, so they're quieter than impact models. They offer fine resolution, almost as good as a laser printer, but the ink has a tendency to smear if you're not careful with fresh printouts. Many of the color printers you see advertised use inkjet technology.

Prices for inkjet printers run from $450 to $800 dollars, depending on speed and other capabilities. Color printers run from $2,000 up.

Daisywheel Printers

Daisywheel printers offer inexpensive letter-quality printing, plus they're impact printers, suitable for forms. The trade-off? They're noisier than a jack-hammer outside your window. They depend on striking a little wheel that spins and searches for each letter embossed upon it, so they're slow. Also, they usually turn up their nose at printing color or graphics. If you're on a budget and need solid, dependable "black and white" output, check out a daisywheel printer. But cover your ears.

In This Chapter, You Learned . . .

A variety of printers exist to help you show your work to others. Dot-matrix printers are fine for average needs, while a laser printer provides high-quality output. Ink-jet printers and daisywheel models both print smart looking documents; ink-jets are capable of graphics and are more expensive, while daisywheel models can print only text and can be purchased quite cheaply.

NOTE

When shopping for a printer, have a friend make up a floppy disk with a brief text file, a small graphics file, and a file from the application you'll use most often. Ask the dealer to print out these files on various types of printers.

Chapter 16 Checklist:

Evaluating Printer Output

Printer Type	Features	Print Quality	Price
_____	_____	_____	_____
_____	_____	_____	_____
_____	_____	_____	_____

Don't Forget to Ask . . .

- Do I need to print images as well as text?
- What speed requirements, if any, must I consider?
- What print quality does my application require?

- Do I need to use special forms or nonstandard paper?
- Do I need color printing?

Notes: _____

_____

_____

_____

_____

_____

_____

_____

_____

_____

_____

_____

_____

chapter

17

Modems

Several of the user scenarios back in Chapter 3 involved sending and receiving information through a PC linked to another computer via modems and an ordinary phone line.

- Ed the accountant uses his home PC to catch up on work he brings home from the office. He plans to use a modem to send completed work back to his office computer. That way he can *telecommute*, or work from home, on days when the traffic's particularly gnarly.

- The Trujillo family enjoys finding new ways to put their home PC to use. They plan to subscribe to an on-line service called Prodigy, where they can meet other families and share similar interests on a variety of *forums*, or discussion areas. A service called CheckFree that offers electronic bill-paying is something else the Trujillos want to investigate.

- Mary the student has decided to hook up a modem to her low-cost PC in order to *download*, or bring into her PC, research materials for her numerous term papers.

- Carl and Susan depend quite a bit on their PC in running their small business. In the evenings, they enjoy relaxing while calling electronic Bulletin Board Systems, or BBSs. They particularly enjoy calling small-business oriented BBSs and discussing issues with other entrepreneurs. Perhaps they'll eventually decide to run their own BBS, so they can automate customer support and find a better way to distribute sales information.

- Leah wouldn't be anywhere without her desktop publishing software, or the high-end, graphics-oriented hardware she's purchased to run it. She particularly enjoys the convenience and economy of using her modem to send completed layouts to a service bureau for color processing.

In this chapter, you'll see how a modem works and how having one can expand your computing experience.

What's a Modem?

A *modem* is a device that enables your computer to exchange information with other computers over ordinary phone lines. Two very different computers can communicate: one might be a sophisticated research-level supercomputer, the other a humble home PC. The two computers don't even have to share the same operating system software. The only requirement is that both computers be attached to a Modulator/Demodulator, or modem for short.

When you're linked to the other computer via modem, you're at least partially in control of that system. If you type your name, it appears on the computer at the other end. That's because the modem *modulates*, or takes apart, the electronic signals from your PC—translating them into audible tones the phone system can understand. Once the tones arrive at the other end, the modem there *demodulates* those phone tones, reassembling them into electronic, digital signals understandable by computers.

External vs. Internal Modems

Modems come in two styles: *external* and *internal*, as Figure 17.1 shows.

External Modems

The advantages of an external modem are that it has a more audible speaker, plus a row of diagnostic lights across the front. Both of these features let you gauge the success of a transmission. The disadvantages are the external modem takes up more desk space; and, because a modem is a serial device, an external modem takes up one of your serial ports to connect to the PC.

A row of lights embellish the front of an external modem, as Figure 17.2 shows. The lights indicate how your transmission's going.

Figure 17.1

You can buy an external or an internal modem.

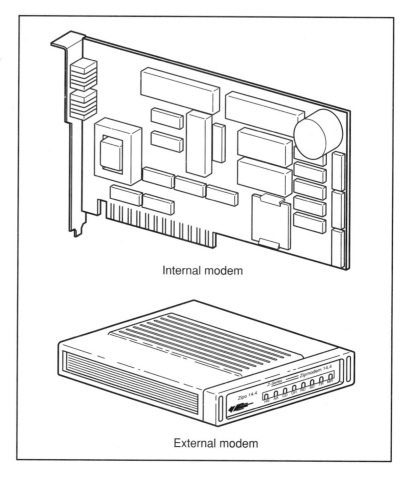

Internal modem

External modem

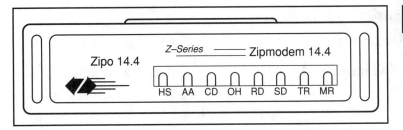

Figure 17.2

External modems come with diagnostic lights along the front.

Diagnostic lights let you watch the modem send and receive data, and you can determine whether a glitch happened because of your computer or the one at the other end. Table 17.1. spells out the letters you'll find next to each light.

Table 17.1   An external modem's lights convey transmission status in a way an internal modem is unable to do.

Label	Stands For . . .	Light Is On When . . .
HS	High-Speed	The modem has achieved its highest transmission rate.
AA	Auto-Answer	The modem is ready to answer an incoming call.
CD	Carrier Detect	The modem has connected with another PC/modem.

continues

Table 17.1   Continued

Label	*Stands For . . .*	*Light Is On When . . .*
OH	Off-Hook	The modem has taken over the phone line; the phone's "off the hook."
RD	Receive Data	The modem is receiving data you've told it to download.
SD	Send Data	The modem is receiving signals from its PC or sending data.
TR	Terminal Ready	The modem is connected to the PC and reads the communication software.
MR	Modem Ready	The modem is powered on, ready to work.

Internal Modems

An internal modem fits into one of your PC's expansion slots, just as any other expansion device. Internal modems cost less than external models, and they take up less space because they're housed in the system box.

Internal modems present certain disadvantages, however. For one, you can't take it with you. An internal modem bought for one type of a Macintosh, for example, can't connect to your IBM PC-compatible computer. Second, the internal modem isn't as outgoing as the external version: It doesn't tell you how it's doing by flashing diagnostic lights, and it uses a muffled, tinny speaker to squeal its joy at reaching a modem at the other end.

Modem Speed

Modems transmit data to other computers in spurts called *bits per second*, or *bps*. You'll see modems rated at 300, 1,200, 2,400 and 9,600 bps—and each new product cycle brings higher speeds. As their speeds rise, so do their prices. Don't even consider buying a modem in the 300 bps range. Even the 1,200 bps model is slow, especially if you're *downloading* (receiving) or *uploading* (sending) a large file.

Jär-gen:

A bit is the smallest unit of data with which your computer works. Eight bits make up one character.

Prices for 2,400 bps modems, starting at around $100, are attractive and make this model the best buy. Of course, there's always the glossy 9,600 bps racehorse gleaming in the corner, complete with a racehorse price tag. And even faster models beckon the unwary shopper. You can end up paying $800 and up for a super-fast, feature-laden modem.

You've heard it before, but buying the best modem for your PC set-up involves determining your needs. If a modem is a central part of your computing plan, of course it makes sense to spring for the fastest, most feature-laden model you can afford.

If a modem is advertised as jumping to the next higher speed when connecting to the same modem type, it's true, under extremely ideal conditions. Don't pay extra for this feature.

Modem Compatibility

As with other segments of the PC industry, compatibility counts in modems, too. Look for modems that support the following standards.

HISTORY

AT Command Set   A modem company called Hayes pioneered something called the *AT command set* (also called the *Hayes command set*). The command set initiated standards in modem communications where none existed before.

Because the AT command set caught on so widely, almost every modem on the market today supports it. Modem-related software, also called communications software, supports it too. So, in order to be able to communicate with another computer/modem, your modem must be compatible with the AT command set—whether you choose a Hayes or another brand of modem.

CCITT Standards

Table 17.2. lists some other modem standards you'll see in ads. These features increase rates of data compression or transmission. You may pay quite a bit extra for one or more of these features, so make sure you actually need them.

Table 17.2   Oft-seen modem standards, known as the CCITT Standards.

Standard	*Capability*
V.32bis	Two modems equipped with this standard can communicate at 14,400 bps.
V.32	A specification for two similarly equipped modems to talk at 9,600 bps.
V.42	The standard for point-to-point error control.
V.42bis	The standard for two similarly equipped modems to compress data, enabling faster transmissions.
MNP 4	A standard for error control, contained also in V.42bis.
MNP 5	A standard for data compression.

Error Correction Is Important

At one time or another, all of us have experienced a lousy phone connection, with so many clicks and gulps both parties agree to hang up and try again (if they make it that far). And then, there are the times when you're talking to someone halfway around the world, and they sound like they're right in your kitchen.

Because modem communications take place over ordinary phone lines, they're subject to the same noises and static as any other phone conversation. In modem terms, this interference is called *line noise.* Normal modems, being the dutiful creatures they are, try to read and interpret line noise as they would any phone signal. Modems with built-in error correction attempt to verify every bit sent and received.

There's one catch: the modem on each end must have *error correction* in order for it to work. Error correcting modems cost more than models without this feature, too. But if your application involves sending and receiving important files, the extra dollars you'll lay out are worth it.

Modem Extras

Many other modem extras increase the speed and the convenience of data communications. Data-compression technology is built into some models. When a modem capable of data compression recognizes that capability in a modem it's connected to, they agree to squeeze down data before sending. Programmable modems can further automate modem sessions. But don't pay too much if programmability is touted

> *Many internal modems come equipped with fax capabilities, for a higher price. You can send and receive faxes while accomplishing other tasks, and there's no need to print the fax out unless you have some reason to keep it.*

BOTTOM LINE

as an extra, for any good communications software can usually accomplish the same things more efficiently.

A host of tiny, portable modems flood the marketplace. These can do double duty on your home or business PC and on any portable computers you may buy in the future.

In This Chapter, You Learned . . .

Modems expand the possibilities of PC ownership. They're rated and priced according to their speed, primarily, although AT-command set compatibility affects both price and performance.

Chapter 17 Checklist:

Brand	Speed	Price	Error Correction?	Extras:
_____	_____	_____	_____	_____
_____	_____	_____	_____	_____
_____	_____	_____	_____	_____
_____	_____	_____	_____	_____
_____	_____	_____	_____	_____

Don't Forget to Ask . . .

- Do my applications require a modem?

- What speed should I buy?

- Do I need extras like portability, programmability, or error correction?

Notes: _____

_____

_____

_____

_____

_____

_____

_____

_____

_____

_____

_____

A Happy Ending

Long ago and far away—way back at the start of this book—we left Bob and Bernice Bungle in some pretty dire straits. Everybody deserves to enjoy their PC to the fullest—even the Bungles of this world—and I'm glad to report that even Bob and Bernice ended up getting "The Most PC for their Money."

It's just that they paid a lot more money than they needed to, since they each hired a PC consultant to untangle the snarls caused by their hasty, unplanned computer purchases. (The funny thing is that each of the consultants sat Bob and Bernice down and took them through the very same buying steps that you completed with just the help of this book!)

First, the consultants pointed out some tedious tasks Bob and Bernice were doing by hand—tasks that their PCs were only too happy to tackle. Then they found software that could take care of those tasks. The good thing is that Bob and Bernice only needed to purchase one or two hardware extras to accommodate the new software's needs—because each had been sold a fairly high-end PC system.

Bernice Makes a Friend (or Two)

Once he helped her with the technical glitch (her PC's monitor wasn't plugged in all the way), Bernice's consultant arranged all the manufacturers' warranty information in one, easily accessible place. He helped her automate her entire business. And he even dug up a "find the Elvis" adventure game called Search for The King to play in her off-hours. (Bernice just *loves* Elvis.)

The consultant urged her to attend the small, general-purpose user group that met in the town hall once a month. And whom did she spot there but Eunice Euler, her prime competitor! Amazingly, once Bernice put away her claws, she found that Eunice was a nice person. In fact, Eunice turned out to be downright helpful, since she'd gone through some of the same trials of automating her small business. And the two women discovered a shared love: Elvis.

Bernice and Eunice decided their small town had plenty of room for two beauty supply shops. They've even schemed on a way to pool some restocking orders, so they can qualify for volume discounts—using their PCs to track inventory, of course.

A Versatile New Family Member

Bob Bungle's consultant urged the entire Bungle family to brainstorm ways to use the new PC. After watching the consultant set up the PC, Bob found that he had a flair for working with utility software and writing small programs of his own. Bob found an island of calm in the precise thinking required by a programming language—a relief, perhaps, from his normally chaotic, scatter-brained ways!

After the family decided to position the new computer in the corner of the den opposite Penny's woodworking tools, Bob's wife found herself gravitating to the PC more often to design projects there—and came to enjoy planning new projects as much as actually building them.

Son Steve has hardly touched the requisite copy of Arkanoid the family bought to toss on the PC. Instead, he's busy creating psychedelic fractal designs on the color monitor, using a commonly available program where advanced mathematical formulas actually show up as graphic images. He's decided to talk to a couple of computer engineers at his school's job fair, to see if that might be a neat career.

Daughter Marsha still enjoys romping with her canine pal Hugo best, but the rest of the family figures that's more time on the PC for them!

Setting Up Your New PC

Bringing a new PC into the home or office can be one of the most exciting events you'll experience—partly because, unlike other major purchases like a car or a refrigerator, there's practically no limit to what a PC can do. Scan the sections below for ways to ensure your new arrival will feel "right at home."

First Thing, Look Inside

Slip under the "hood" to make sure you got what you paid for. Removing a PC's case is quite easy—they all vary but they've improved quite a bit over the old-style cases you had to practically pry off. If you already fired it up in that first rush of glorious enthusiasm, turn it off before attempting to look inside; shut off peripherals first and then switch off the system box. Then make sure they're all unplugged. Don't let any screws get lost in the carpet, either.

Peek at the add-in boards, and ensure they fit without crowding. Make sure the hard disk brand, printed on the drive, is the one you specified. Look at the memory chips to see that they're the right speed and in the right amount. Shoot a glance over at the microprocessor, just to make sure it's the one advertised in your system. Count the expansion slots left over after configuring your system with the video card. Look at that, too—make sure it's the high-end, color-extravaganza card you paid for, complete with any video memory chips you added onto it. And finally, glance at the FCC certification sticker. It should wear a scarlet "B."

Consider Comfort When Deciding Where to Put It

The PC's accessibility and convenience are important factors in deciding where to put it, but think comfort, too. Some of the best computer nooks I've seen are modeled after Navy ship control consoles, with low room lighting and everything within arm's reach.

Lighting

Make sure any window light that falls on the screen can be shielded with curtains or blinds. There should be a light source at right angles to the monitor, and any lamps should be adjustable, as well as dimmable. Viewing angle is crucial to head and neck comfort—and your vision stamina. Try for a 60-degree viewing angle, if possible.

Desk and Chair

Depending on your height, the desk should be 24-inches to 30-inches high for optimum arm comfort. Take my word and buy a wrist protector pad. Make sure the keyboard's angled with a slightly upward tilt.

Of course, the computer chair is one of the most important factors in the ergonomics equation—you'll be in it the whole time you're using your PC. Look for an adjustable chair with a 5-prong base for security.

The seat should swivel and sport, at least, a 1-inch padding on the bottom. Some users speak highly of tilting seats that angle slightly forward and relieve pressure on the back and thighs (once you get used to the feeling that you're sliding off it). Consider arm rests for the times you're not actually typing—they take pressure off your neck and shoulders.

Prepare Your PC

Make sure everything is already plugged in and ready to go: Save all the cartons and Styrofoam reinforcements in case something needs to be shipped. It's best to lure one of the computer store techs over with a bag of Oreos to set up your system for you. Make sure you know how to start and exit each of the applications you'll be using.

Have the tech show you how to find two essential files: AUTOEXEC.BAT and CONFIG.SYS. While you're at it, print out their contents—you might have to read this information over the phone to a software or hardware support staffer someday. Each time these files are changed, as with the addition of a new mouse or another device, for example, print out a new copy and keep it handy. Print out a copy of your system setup information, as well.

Enjoy!

Despite the effort it took to buy the best PC for your needs, this is only the beginning. I'm glad to say that what lies ahead is the fun part: using and becoming productive on your new PC! Enjoy the process, and help spread the word: PCs are fun stuff!

Glossary

While tracking down the best PC for your money, you're sure to spend hours in deep discussions with computer store clerks and mail-order sales representatives. Sidestep the jargon they're bound to toss out by turning to the listings in these pages.

132-column carriage   extra-wide dot-matrix printer feature.

24-pin printer   high-end dot-matrix printer; prints true near-letter quality output.

286   nickname for 80286-powered PC or chip that bosses one around.

3 1/2-inch disk   micro floppy disk enclosed in hard plastic case; comes in double and high density, fancy words for the simple fact that one holds more than the other (1.4M versus 720K).

386   nickname for 80386 chip; a 386-based PC.

386DX   full-fledged 80386 chip; a PC powered by one.

386SX   386 chip with external bus disabled so it's more affordable; a PC driven by one.

486   nickname for 80486 chip; a 486-based PC.

486DX   full-fledged 80486 chip; a PC powered by one.

486DX2/50   one of a recent series of chips from Intel Corp. that doubles a PC's processing speed for internal chip tasks; ominously known as The Doubler.

486SX   486 chip with math coprocessor disabled so it's more affordable; a PC that sports this chip.

5 1/4-inch disk   floppy disk enclosed in semi-hard plastic coating; comes in two capacities, or densities: 1.2M and 360K.

80-column carriage   the carriage-width on a standard-width dot-matrix printer.

80286   older chip, or PC powered by this chip; the first AT (advanced technology) PC driven by this chip.

80386   the 80386 microprocessor; PC based on this chip.

80486   the 80486 microprocessor; PC bossed around by this chip.

80586   there won't be one; Intel's calling it the P5 or some other funky name, for copyright purposes.

8080   honorable ancestor of today's 80x86 microprocessor/PC family.

8086 early IBM PC-compatible chip; a PC driven by one.

8088 powered the first true IBM-brand PC; a PC powered by one.

80x86 the microprocessor family of the IBM PC-compatibles.

9-pin printer low-cost, low-resolution dot-matrix printer.

A

add-on board an expansion board; a new device may come with one; so do upgrades like memory boards or hard disk cards; fits into a spare slot in the expansion bus.

app short for application software.

application another name for software; suggests more the task or problem to be solved by the software: a word-processing application, for example.

arrow keys see *cursor movement keys*.

AT-compatible said of software or hardware that works with '286-class or later-model PCs; oddly, even though the 80286 was the first AT, 80386 and above computers fall into the AT-clan as well.

B

back up to copy data or programs onto floppy disks or storage media other than the hard drive, for safekeeping.

basic input-output system (BIOS) a PC's permanent start-up instructions, found on the motherboard's ROM chips.

baud used interchangeably (to be picky, wrongly) for bps to measure a modem's transmission speed; actually measures the number of transitions in the modem signal per second; from J.M.E. Baudot, French telegraphy wizard.

BBS see *Bulletin Board System*.

Bernice a mail-order maladroit; owns the biggest doorstop in town.

binary digit abbreviated as bit; the smallest unit of data a PC processes; bits are actually switches, either 1s or 0s—on or off—in the binary, or base 2, number system.

BIOS see *Basic Input/Output System*.

bit short for binary digit, the smallest unit of info a PC processes at any one time.

bite computers don't, contrary to popular opinion; also, pronunciation of byte, data quantity.

bits per second (bps) measures rate of data movement to and from CPU and other components; also measures speed of modem transmissions.

board 1. nickname for expansion board, a way to add new devices to a PC; 2. short for BBS, or Bulletin Board System.

booting up   starting a PC; powering it up; turning it on.

bootstrapping   the "start-up" process a PC goes through when it's turned on.

bps   see *bits per second.*

buffer   a place in memory to store data temporarily, while it's waiting to print, for example.

Bulletin Board System (BBS)   a hobbyist's computer running special software and one or more modems; modem enthusiasts enjoy calling BBSs for news, social interaction, and recreation.

bundled   packaged as part of a PC system; can be software, or hardware extras like a mouse.

bus   the system architecture, especially the data path and expansion slot design, of the motherboard; circuitry on a PC's motherboard by which data travels to and from the microprocessor.

bus mouse   a mouse that connects to a PC through an expansion card.

byte   measure of data quantity: eight bits make a byte; more commonly seen in thousands, kilobyte; millions, megabyte; or even billions, gigabyte.

C

cache memory   chips that store frequently used data to speed up CPU access and thus, processing time.

card   see *expansion card.*

cathode ray tube (CRT)   the guts of a monitor (or TV set).

CD-ROM   short for Compact Disc-Read Only Memory; CD-ROM discs store software and are read by CD-ROM drives you attach to your PC; you can't copy data, or "write" to one; this increasingly popular method of software distribution enables big, piggy software to grow even bigger, piggier.

central processing unit (CPU)   primary chip, or microprocessor, inside a PC.

CGA   short for color graphics adapter, an early, crude color display technology; refers to monitor; also refers to adapter card that powers the monitor.

characters per second (cps)   measures a dot matrix printer's speed.

chip   nickname for microprocessor, the silicon engines of computing; not necessarily the main chip, or CPU.

Class A rating   FCC approval rating for work-site-only PCs.

Class B rating   FCC approval rating for home PCs, more stringent than Class A; this rating won't cause as much radio interference (and neighbor interference!).

click   to press-and-release a mouse's button; software often directs you to click on a command to activate it.

clip art   digitized graphics; used for adding pictures to a document; many software packages come with clip art bundled inside.

clock speed   the basic operating speed of a microprocessor, measured in megahertz (MHz).

clone   a copy; usually refers to an IBM PC-compatible, but video cards, mice, software, almost any product can be a clone of a more famous, or standard, brand.

clusters   groupings of files on a floppy or hard disk.

cold boot   to power-on a PC; turn it off and on again after a system crash (hard on the system and to be avoided).

COM   see *communications port.*

communications port   COM, or serial port; named for the communications devices called modems that plug into these. Typically seen as COM1, COM2, and so on.

configuration   a PC's particular hardware set up; sometimes, software set up.

controller   mechanism on a hard drive that tells it what to do; determines hard drive's type.

conventional memory   The first 640K of memory in a PC.

convergence   perfect alignment of electron gun beam and shadow mask; this video-display nirvana produces high-quality monitor image.

cps   see *characters per second.*

CPU   see *central processing unit.*

crash   short for system crash, from hard disk heads *crash*ing onto platters; the PC goes down, and everything comes to a halt until the system's rebooted; can be caused by hardware or by software.

CRT   see *cathode ray tube.*

cursor   the blinking typing point or "hot spot" on-screen.

cursor movement keys   keys that move the cursor. Most keyboards feature four arrow keys: up, down, left and right; four other keys, home, pg up, pg dn, and end, move the cursor, too.

D

daisywheel printer   impact printer; works by striking hammer on spinning letter wheel.

data   information used by a PC; also, data files are your work in a software program, as opposed to the program files themselves.

data bus   circuitry on a PC's motherboard by which data travels to and from the microprocessor.

daughterboard   another name for expansion card.

device   a monitor, keyboard, mouse, or any peripheral that can connect to a PC.

dinosaur   older PC model no longer sold or supported with software; see *XT*.

DIP switches   toggle switches found on the motherboard and on expansion cards; they control settings you manipulate by "flipping" the switch.

disc   fancy word for disk, used with CD-ROM discs.

disk   data storage media; see *floppy disk, hard disk*.

disk operating system (DOS)   software that runs the PC's basic functions; other software's added on top of an operating system; typically abbreviated

DOS; often seen as the brand-name MS-DOS, for Microsoft Disk Operating System, the most widely-used brand; OS/2 and UNIX are two of many PC-level alternates to MS-DOS.

diskette   nickname for floppy disk; comes in two sizes, four capacities.

DOS   see *disk operating system*.

dot pitch   qualitative measure of a monitor; determines picture focus; here, smaller numbers mean better quality.

dot matrix   system of pin arrangement on printhead of dot-matrix printer; this printer family.

dots per inch (dpi)   measure of resolution on monitors and printer output quality; higher is better.

double-density disk   sounds like a big deal, but really just a lower capacity floppy; comes in two versions: 5 1/4-inch version holds 360K and 3 1/2-inch version holds 720K of data.

double click   two rapid, successive mouse clicks.

Doubler   a series of CPUs that can double a PC's processing rate for certain tasks.

download   to bring data into a PC through a modem or serial connection.

downloadable font   printer lettering style, stored in software form.

downward compatible   works with older models of like components: a Super VGA monitor is downward compatible with a CGA video card (shiver).

dpi   see *dots per inch.*

draft mode   quality of printout acceptable for a rough draft.

DRAM   see *dynamic RAM.*

drive bays   horizontal carriers in the system box for hard and floppy drives.

driver   small program file that communicates a new device's configuration and set up requirements to the PC's operating system and other software.

DX2/n   recent chip model that doubles PC processing to *n* speed for internal microprocessor functions.

Dynamic RAM (DRAM)   a variety of memory chip.

E

EGA   short for enhanced graphics adapter; semi-early color display technology; refers to monitor and to adapter card that powers the monitor.

EISA   abbreviation for enhanced ISA, an enhanced model of system-bus architecture.

emulation   to copy, act like; a hardware device, such as a printer, can emulate a more standard printer brand, for example.

enhanced keyboard   keyboard with separate arrow keys; function keys along top.

Enter key   on PC's keyboard, works like carriage-return, or to invoke commands in software.

environment   a program that runs on top of DOS to help you avoid direct communication with DOS itself.

ESDI   fast hard disk controller; found on high-end, large hard drives.

Eunice   Bernice's nemesis.

expanded memory   RAM added through an expansion card on 286 PCs and lower or through software on 386 PCs and above; a Good Thing, because software makes use of all the spare memory it can get its greedy little hands on.

expansion bus   system of expansion slots on a PC's motherboard; individual PCs vary in bus architecture; it's essential to look for an expansion bus that allows for sufficient additions later.

expansion card   an add-on card for a new device like spare memory, a mouse or a modem, for example; fits into a spare slot in the expansion bus.

expansion slot   slot on the motherboard's expansion bus where you add expansion cards; PCs average five spare slots—more is better.

extended memory   usable memory over 640K.

external data path   conduit for data from microprocessor to system memory and expansion bus; partially disabled on the 80386SX chip.

F

file   the work you do on a PC, a program or other data is stored in files on a floppy or hard disk, or on other storage media.

fixed   nonremovable, as in fixed disk, for hard disk.

flash BIOS   this unusual feature allows the ROM BIOS to be updated, electronically, to reflect hardware upgrades and other changes to a PC's configuration.

floppy   short for floppy disk, also diskette; removable media that stores data for use on a PC; comes in two sizes, four capacities.

floppy disk drive   mechanical device inside system box which reads from and writes to floppy disks.

font   style of lettering, form of type style; used in comparing a printer's capability to use different type styles; each bold, italic, or heavy version of a type style is a separate typeface, or font, from the old photo-typesetting days; increasingly, and wrongly, coming to mean type family.

font cartridge   plug-in printer cartridge that adds new fonts to a printer.

forums   discussion areas focusing on specific topics on electronic bulletin board systems or commercial on-line services.

freezing up   the PC refuses to work; system crash.

function keys   keys on PC keyboard not found on a typewriter; perform various operations depending on software in use.

G

game card   expansion card containing a special port for a joystick to plug into.

game port   a special port on a game card for attaching a joystick.

GB   see *gigabyte*.

gigabyte   roughly a billion bytes.

graphical user interface (GUI)   presents a way of using computers through activating pictures, or icons, that represent commands, programs and files.

graphics   images, charts, clip art; the programs and peripherals that let you use graphics, as in graphics printer.

graphics card   expansion card that runs a monitor.

GUI   pronounced *gooey*. See *graphical user interface*.

H

hand-held scanner   device that transforms an image into digital data with which PCs can work.

hard disk drive   mass storage device for a PC to safeguard programs and data.

hardcopy   a printout; paper copy you can carry around to show off your documents or other PC labors.

hardware   any equipment that can be used in a PC configuration, from the PC itself to peripherals, like a music synthesizer.

Hercules graphics adapter (HGC)   a monochrome graphics standard.

HGC   see *Hercules graphics adapter*.

high-density disk   high-capacity floppy disk; comes in two versions: 5 1/4-inch version holds 1.2M and 3 1/2-inch version holds 1.4M.

I

IBM PC-compatible   works with computers or chips of the IBM PC family; also, a PC that sports a nationally-recognized brand-name, like Compaq. See *clone*.

icons   graphic representations of programs, files, or commands on a PC; seen in GUI software or on Macintosh PCs.

IDE   one type of hard disk controller, common in mid-range, low-cost drives.

impact printer   on these, the print mechanism strikes the print carriage; usually noisier than non-impact variety.

inkjet printer   a nonimpact printer that works by shooting ink blobs through dots.

input device   any of a group of mechanisms to input information to a PC; keyboard, mouse, joystick, microphone, and so on.

interface card   serial or parallel board, also multifunction board; usually already bundled inside PCs.

interlaced   a monitor whose electron beams scan alternating lines; older technology; causes flicker that results in eye-fatigue.

internal data path   one of a microprocessor's two data "hoses"; data moves around and processed within the CPU via this path.

ISA   the original system bus architecture of the AT-model PC; still a viable standard.

J

joystick   pointing device used primarily to blow up invading spacecraft and other bad guys; these vary in quality: don't bother unless you get a good one.

K

K   abbreviation for kilobyte, approximately one-thousand bytes.

key   unit on a keyboard; also, to type, or key, something into a computer.

kilobyte   approximately one-thousand bytes, abbreviated as K, more rarely seen as KB.

L

laptop   small, portable PC weighing less than 15 pounds, generally powered by batteries; notebook computers are lighter, smaller laptops.

laser printer   nonimpact printer that works similarly to a photocopier; this expensive, fast, high-quality printer drove thousands of innocent people to desktop publishing.

letter-quality   high-quality printer output, as opposed to near-letter quality or draft mode.

line printer port (LPT)   another name for parallel port; more commonly seen abbreviated and numbered, as in LPT1, LPT2, and so on.

local bus   enhanced expansion bus circuitry that provides direct data exchange between the CPU and expansion cards, speeding operation of that device; not widely supported and limited to video cards, for now.

LPT   see *line printer port*.

M

Macintosh   the other leading PC family; often shortened to Mac; strangely, its slogan is "The computer for the rest of us," even though the IBM PC-compatible family has a much larger software base and user population.

Macintosh-compatible   works with a Macintosh PC.

math coprocessor   an add-on chip that takes some of the load off the microprocessor by performing arithmetic functions and graphics processing; not every motherboard sports a slot for a math coprocessor; the 486DX has one built in.

matrix   an array; often seen describing the arrangement of pins on dot-matrix printer.

MB   see *megabyte*.

MCA   abbreviation for micro-channel architecture, IBM's version of an enhanced system bus architecture; see *EISA, ISA*.

MDA   early monochrome monitor/video card standard.

megabyte (M or MB)   roughly 1 million bytes of data; more often seen as M or MB.

megahertz (MHz)   1 million hertz, or clock cycles per second; measures speed of CPU.

memory   generally refers to volatile memory, or RAM, where a PC's microprocessor stores data temporarily; ROM, a permanent set of PC housekeeping instructions, is another type of memory.

memory cache   chips that form a holding zone for frequently used data; speeds up CPU access and thus, processing time.

menu   a list of choices or range of commands in a software program.

MHz   see *megahertz*.

micro floppy   official name for 3 1/2-inch disks.

microcomputer   official name for the entire PC species, including Macs, Amigas, Ataris, and every other PC family.

microprocessor   official name of the CPU, or main PC chip; brains behind a PC.

millisecond   one-thousandth of a second; measures hard disk access speed, for one.

MIPS   short for millions of instructions per second; speed rating for CPU processing

instructions; differs from megahertz, rating a chip's clock speed.

modem   short for modulator/demodulator (you can see why they came up with a shorter name); scrambles a PC's data to enable transmission over ordinary phone lines, where a modem at the other end unscrambles data to be understandable to that PC.

monitor   PC's video display unit; can be color or monochrome and capable of any of several video standards.

monochrome   single-color, refers to monitor display; usually amber or green on black.

motherboard   a large, green printed circuit board carpeting the system box; provides framework for the CPU, expansion bus, memory chips, and all other parts of a PC.

mouse   *Mus musculus*, family *muridae*, order *rodentia*; also, pointing device, more resembling bar soap than creature; comes in serial and bus, optical and mechanical, and corded or cordless species.

mouse pad   pad used for rolling a mouse over; comes in plain rubbery form, for mechanical mice, and optically readable, gridded form for optical mice.

mouse pen   pointing device shaped like an oversized pen with roller ball on bottom and buttons similar to a mouse's.

MS-DOS   abbreviation for Microsoft Disk Operating System, the most common operating system seen on IBM PC-compatibles.

multi-frequency   monitor capable of switching to nearly any video mode.

multi-function card   expansion card containing multiple ports, usually a parallel and two serial ports, sometimes a game port, too; generally, at least one comes bundled inside a PC system.

multi-scan   another name for *multi-frequency.*

multisync   same thing as *multi-frequency.*

N

N-key rollover test   one way to check a keyboard's quality.

near-letter quality (NLQ)
midrange printout quality; almost letter quality; one standard for measuring printer output.

NLQ   see *near-letter quality.*

non-impact printer   laser, inkjet, and other printer technologies that don't involve

the striking of a printhead or hammer to produce printed output; quieter than impact printers.

non-interlaced   monitor technology where inner monitor surface is scanned all at once by electron beams instead of in alternating sections as with older, interlaced models; minimizes flicker and eyestrain.

numeric keypad   dual-function PC keyboard area, located on keyboard's left, housing a matrix of number keys and operands in a layout similar to a calculator's; eases numeric input and arithmetic computing applications; arrow, or cursor movement keys found here, too.

NumLock   PC keyboard key that toggles the numeric keypad between numeric or arrow key (cursor-movement) mode.

O

on-line service   any commercial service accessible via modem; CompuServe, Prodigy, GEnie, and America On-line are a few examples.

operating system   see *disk operating system.*

OS   short for operating system. See *disk operating system.*

OS/2   alternate PC operating system to MS-DOS; although in development many years now, has been slow in catching on.

P

pages per minute (ppm)   measure of a laser printer's output speed; for printing multiple copies of the same page, 6 ppm is the average.

palette   monitor/video card term for the total, maximum numbers of colors possible; only a fraction of the card's palette can be seen at any one time.

parallel interface card   expansion card that adds parallel ports to a PC.

parallel port   extension of the PC's expansion bus; enables parallel devices to be connected to the PC; often called printer port.

PC   see *personal computer.*

PC-clone   See *clone.*

PC-compatible   PC from a line of name-brand, nationally distributed PCs, like Dell or Compaq; see *clone.*

peripherals   general term for any devices outside the actual PC system box: includes monitors, keyboards, pointing devices, music keyboards, and, by extension, the expansion cards needed to run any of these devices.

personal computer (PC)   common name for the microcomputer family of computers; more generally, has come to mean IBM-compatible family of microcom-puters, even though Mac-, Amiga- or Atari-brand microcomputers, technically, are also PCs.

pixel   short for picture element; the smallest part of an image on a PC's monitor, likened to a dot; the more pixels a monitor displays going across and down, the tighter the monitor's focus, or resolution.

pointing device   peripherals that input data into a PC; used in conjunction with a keyboard to enhance precision in navigating through software.

points per inch (ppi)   gauges mouse agility. A higher number means a more sensitive mouse.

portable computer   loose term for any PC that can be carried around; ranges from heavy, 15-pound luggables to tiny palmtop PCs weighing less than a pound.

ports   gateways to your PC's innards so devices can connect to it; see *serial ports, SCSI* and *parallel ports.*

PostScript   page-description language used with sophisticated laser printers.

power strip   extension cord-like device fitted with eight or so sockets; something you forget to buy and have to run out to the store for, once you get your PC home and set up.

power surge   fluctuations in electrical current that can be dastardly to your data.

power supply   metal box inside the system box that supplies power to the PC; sports a fan for cooling purposes.

ppi   see *points per inch.*

ppm   see *pages per minute.*

printer   device that lets you print your work; most commonly attaches to parallel port; enables you to share "hardcopy" printouts with others.

printhead   printer mechanism that strikes ribbon and paper.

processor   short for microprocessor; also CPU or just chip.

program   short for software program; also application software; the special files full of data and instructions that make your PC do something; also, verb: to write computer-readable code that makes a PC do what you want.

programming languages   any of several very precise, artificial languages with which you can write your own computer programs.

R

RAM   see *random access memory.*

RAM cache   see *cache memory.*

random-access memory (RAM)   volatile memory used as a temporary data storage tank by the micro-processor; disappears into thin air when computer's shut off.

read-only memory (ROM)   a set of permanent instructions that tell a computer how to coordinate its various components and get to work; contains system's BIOS.

refresh rate   monitor's vertical electron scan rate; faster scanning ensures less flicker.

removable media   PC file storage media that can be carried around, like a floppy disk or CD-ROM disc as opposed to a fixed hard disk.

reset button   button on outside of PC's system box that lets you restart the PC without turning off its power.

resolution   measure of image quality; determines focus and overall picture sharpness; used in comparing video cards and the monitors they control, as well as the output of printers and scanners.

ROM   see *read-only memory.*

RS-232 port   another name for serial port; deriving from an industry standard for typical connectors to the port.

S

scan rate   two types, vertical and horizontal scan rate, determine the monitor's overall quality; higher rates make for a better picture, less flicker and less eyestrain.

scanner   device for digitizing and inputting graphics into a PC; resulting images can then be incorporated into party flyers, computer art, and other creations.

SCSI   (small computer system interface): pronounced scuzzy; nearly always abbreviated as SCSI. A high-end interface you can buy and add to a PC's expansion bus; accommodates SCSI devices like high-capacity hard drives or CD-ROM players; faster than the more commonly bundled parallel and serial interfaces under certain conditions.

select   to use a mouse or cursor key combination to highlight text or commands in software.

serial interface card   provides a computer with a serial port where serial devices like modems can attach; goes in PC's expansion bus.

serial mouse   pointing device that comes with no expansion card; instead it connects to a serial port on the PC.

serial port   connects to the motherboard by means of a serial interface card; provides a place to connect serial printers, mice and modems, among other serial devices, to your PC; most PCs come bundled with at least two serial ports.

shadow RAM   sounds like a character in a '40s radio serial, but it's really just a feature to speed microprocessor access to the BIOS instructions by loading these into fast RAM at boot-up.

shareware   although not free, this type of software's okay to share with others; a try-before-you-buy marketing concept that depends on the honor system for payment to software's authors.

silicon   material most commonly used in making computer chips.

slot   short for expansion slot; raised, narrow opening in PC's expansion bus where you plug in expansion cards; can be 8-bits, 16-bits, or 32-bits in length.

small computer system interface   see *SCSI.*

software   programs to make the computer do an enormous, dazzling variety of tasks. See *programs.*

sound card   peripheral you can buy to add sound capabilities to a PC.

ST-506   older, slower hard drive controller.

stacked drive   1. disk drive stacked on another in a vertical drive bay configuration; 2. hard drive on which the data's been compressed using one of several commercial compression utilities.

Stacker   a popular data compression product; comes in hardware (expansion card) and software versions.

standard keyboard   PC keyboard that improved upon the original IBM PC model but was largely replaced by the enhanced keyboard.

Star Trek   the first TV series with this name was better.

static RAM   a type of memory chip; faster than DRAM chips.

super VGA   graphics mode that, right now, is quickly becoming the high-end standard; refers both to video card and to monitor models.

surge protection   precaution against electrical current fluctuations that can harm a PC or at least destroy work in progress that hasn't been backed up to a disk; surge protector units are sold in computer stores.

system box   the hard plastic case enclosing a PC's motherboard, power supply, disk drives, and other components.

T

telecommute   work at home enabled by modem that can transfer work to and from the office PC; named for the *telephone* lines that the data transmits over.

tower   vertical system box—usually large—with plenty of expansion slots and drive bays and an oversized power supply to cool all the goodies you can pack inside.

trackball   pointing device housing a mounted ball and adjacent buttons; cursor manipulated by rolling the fingertips across ball and pressing, or clicking, buttons.

tractor-feed paper   printer paper that features continuous-feed holes along the side edges that accommodate the pins of a tractor-feed paper-advancement mechanism.

turbo mode   the faster of a computer's operating speeds.

typeface   technical term for lettering; each bold, italic, or heavy version of a type style is a separate typeface, or font; term hails from the old photo-typesetting days.

U

UNIX   operating system seen infrequently on PCs; fiercely beloved and defended by users, usually researchers, scientists, and engineers.

upgrade   to boost the power and versatility of a component or an entire PC by adding memory chips, a math coprocessor, a bigger hard disk drive, or other upgrades.

uploading   sending information from your PC to another PC through a serial device like a modem; see *downloading*.

user group   group of computer users who meet regularly to share information and experiences about computers; some groups focus on a particular software package or hardware device—others on any common ground, from professional affiliation to computing for people of differing abilities; highly recommended way of snooping-before-shopping for a PC.

utilities   software family designed to beef-up any (sometimes many) of a PC's deficiencies; virus-scanning software is an example of a utility; differs from other software in that it doesn't necessarily aim to accomplish your task but instead tries to make the computer generally more efficient.

V

vertical scanning frequency   a monitor's refresh rate; higher frequencies reduce annoying flicker.

very-large-scale integration (VLSI)   the engineering technology that has enabled dense circuitry on microprocessors, motherboards, and other computer hardware, and thus faster, more capable components.

VESA   video-card manufacturer consortium that sets standards for high-end video modes.

VGA   acronym for video graphics array; high-resolution monitor/video card standard.

video-adapter card   expansion card essential to operating a PC video display, or monitor.

video display   another name for monitor, the screen of a PC system.

viruses   programs written to intentionally destroy the computer or software of another, devised and implemented by maladjusted people.

volatile memory   RAM, which empties itself when its electrical source is cut off (when the PC's turned off or accidentally unplugged, or as the result of a power surge or system crash).

W

wait state   the time a computer spends between instructions waiting for something to do.

window   programs run in boxes, or windows, in Microsoft Windows and other GUIs and even in some non-GUI programs like DESQview, an alternative PC operating environment.

Windows   Microsoft Windows, a graphical user environment where users point at pictures, or icons, instead of typing text to invoke commands.

X

XT-compatible compatible with the original IBM XT computer; this model of computer, or an XT-clone.

Z

zero wait-state a PC with this feature probably sports a RAM cache that reduces the time a computer spends between instructions waiting for something to do.

Index

Symbols

3.5 inch disks/disk drives, 142-145
386DX microprocessors, 82-85
386SX microprocessors, 82-83
486DX microprocessor, 83-84, 282
486DX2 microprocessors, 86, 282
486SX microprocessor, 83-84, 282
5.25 inch disks/disk drives, 142-145
80x86 microprocessors, 71-72
8514/A video standard, 200

A

add-on board, 283
Advanced Micro Devices (AMD)
   microprocessors, 73-75
Ami Pro word processing program, 55
anti-glare coatings, 187
AT command set, 269
AT-compatible keyboards, 214
average access time, 161

B

basic input-output system (BIOS), 283
baud, 283

BBS
   see bulletin board system
BIOS (basic input-output system), 96, 283
   flash BIOS, 88, 288
booting up, 284
buffers, 284
Bulletin Board System (BBS), 284
   mail-order computer support, 25, 26
buses, 100-102, 284
   EISA (Expanded Industry Standard
      Architecture), 100-102, 287
   ISA (Industry Standard Architecture),
      100-102, 289
   local bus, 103
   MCA (MicroChannel Architecture),
      100-102, 290
bus mouse, 227, 284
buying computers
   mail-order, 19-26
   software, 35-38
   stores, 11-15
bytes, 109-110

C

caches/cache memory, 84-85, 113-114,
   284, 291
   hard disks/disk drives, 166, 167
capacity
   floppy disks, 143-145
   hard disks, 160-161
cases, 129-133
cathode ray tubes (CRT), 178, 284

N

O

P

Instructions for Buyer's Checklist

Each chapter presented a checklist of questions and points to consider when shopping. Use the chapter checklists to fill out Section I. Then tear out this card, and make several copies of it, one for each vendor that you're planning to investigate.

Then you're ready to shop! At each store you visit or each mail order dealer you call, fill out Section II to describe the system being offered. (You can usually ask a salesperson to fill it out for you.) You can then bring all the copies home and compare them to decide which is your ideal system.

BUYER'S CHECKLIST

SECTION I: THE SYSTEM THAT I WANT

Processor: _____ 286 _____ 386SX _____ 386 _____ 486SX _____ 486

Chip Speed: _____

Monitor Size/Type: _____

Video Card Type: _____

Hard Disk Size/Type: _____

Floppy Drives: _____ 3.5" _____ 5.25" _____ Both

Other Special Features Desired: _____

_____

_____

_____

Printer: _____ Dot Matrix _____ Inkjet _____ Laser

Printer Features Desired: _____

_____

SECTION II To be filled out when shopping

Vendor Name/Location/Phone

_____

_____

Warranty Terms: _____

_____

In-Home Service Included? _____ Yes _____ No

30-day Money Back Return Offered? _____ Yes _____ No

Restocking Fee Charged? _____ Yes _____ No

Credit Card Payment Fee? _____ Yes _____ No

Chip Brand Name/Type/Speed: _____

Math Coprocessor included? _____ Yes _____ No $_____ extra

BIOS version and make: _____

Upgradable motherboard? _____ Yes _____ No

Remaining Slots after Configuration (size and number of each)

_____

RAM included: _____ RAM Capacity on Motherboard: _____

Type/speed of RAM chips used: _____

RAM cache included? _____ Yes _____ No

Shadow RAM Included? _____ Yes _____ No

Number of Ports: _____ Serial _____ Parallel

Number of Drive Bays: _____

Power Supply Wattage: _____

Other Ports (SCSI, Game, Mouse): _____

Floppy drives included: _____ 3.5" _____ 5.25" H

High Density Floppy drives? _____ Yes _____ No

Number and size of open drive bays: _____

Size/Brand of Hard Drive Included: _____

Hard Drive Controller type: _____

Speed Access/Transfer: _____

MTBF rating: _____

(If applicable) Price to Upgrade to Desired Size/Type: $ _____

Monitor: ____ Included ____ Extra Charge $ _____

Make/Model Number: _____

Type/Size: _____

Maximum Resolution: _____ Dot Pitch: _____

Refresh Rate: _____ Non-Interlaced? ____ Yes ____ No

If Multiscan, how many modes? _____

Video Card Make/Model Number and Type: _____

_____

Video RAM Included: _____ Upgradable to:_____

Maximum Resolution/Mode: _____

Total color Palette: _____ Colors At Once: _____

Card bit-width: _____

Keyboard type included: _____

Price for extended or special model: $_____

Keyboard performance on touch test: ___ Good ___ Fair ___ Poor

N-key rollover test: ___ Good ___ Fair ___ Poor

Enter key accessibility: ___ Good ___ Fair ___ Poor

Modem: ____ Included? ____ Extra Charge? $ _____

Type: ____ Internal ____ External

Speed: ____ 1200 ____ 2400 ____ 9600

Mouse: ____ Included? ____ Extra Charge? $ _____

Type: _____

Special Features: _____

Printer: ____ Included? ____ Extra Charge? $ _____

Type: _____

Special Features: _____

Maintenance/Upkeep Costs per Year: $_____

Operating system software included? ____ Yes ____ No

Installed and configured? Manuals? ____ Yes ____ No

Other software included:

_____ Regular Price: $ _____

_____ Regular Price: $ _____

_____ Regular Price: $ _____

Base System Cost: $_____

Cost Including All Desired Options: $_____

Salesperson _____

Phone Number: _____